Praise for *Less Hustle, More Happy*

'Eureka moments, revelations, clarity and empowerment – that is what you can expect by reading *Less Hustle, More Happy*. In a way that only Claire Seeber could deliver, this book is the most engaging career game plan around. Claire breaks the steps down into bite-sized chunks through personal stories, practical examples and punchy research all weaved together with real language and the fun factor. If you are in any way unsure or unfulfilled in your career, this book is a must-read!'
Ashley McGrath | Chief Executive Officer, CEOs for Gender Equity

'Finally, a book that speaks directly to the struggles many of us face in our careers! This is a game-changer for anyone who's ever felt torn between chasing success and preserving their wellbeing. I personally have suffered the "work harder, sacrifice everything" mentality, and this book is everything I wish I had years ago. Claire is practical, relatable, and so generous in her knowledge and wisdom. Thanks Claire!'
Jodi Geddes | Co-Founder at Well and Circle In, 2022 Telstra Business Awards Winner, 2023 Top 100 Innovators List

'You'll refer back to this book time and time again throughout your career to reflect on the things that are important to you, ask yourself the challenging but necessary questions, and follow Claire's simple and effective framework. Whatever your pursuit, this book will provide you with a pathway to being fulfilled.'
Jodi Paton | Chief People Officer, The Hoyts Group

'Your career is too long and life's too short to be miserable at work. If you want to build your dream career without the hustle, this is your next read. The time to invest in your career is now. The tool to do it is this book.'
Shelley Johnson | Owner of Boldside Consulting and host of the *This is work* podcast

'*Less Hustle, More Happy* is the wake-up call we need, a timely reminder that it's possible to get ahead in our careers without costing our soul or losing our light. This book is a career manifesto for living and working in full colour. Apply the lessons and formulas Claire unpacks in this book now and I promise you'll save yourself a lot of pain, frustration and disappointment later in your career.'
Shane Michael Hatton | Team culture expert and

Less Hustle, More Happy

Less Hustle, More Happy

Be seen, valued
and fulfilled at work
without selling your soul

Claire Seeber

MAJOR
STREET

For my parents, who raised me to have grit and determination, but always love and compassion in my heart.

I am where I am because of you.

First published in 2024 by Major Street Publishing Pty Ltd

info@majorstreet.com.au | majorstreet.com.au

© Claire Seeber 2024

The moral rights of the author have been asserted.

 A catalogue record for this book is available from the National Library of Australia

Printed book ISBN: 978-1-923186-17-0

Ebook ISBN: 978-1-923186-18-7

Cover design by Typography Studio

Internal design by Production Works

Printed in Australia by Griffin Press

10 9 8 7 6 5 4 3 2 1

Contents

Preface

I have a photo of me as a young girl that I love. I am dressed up in my favourite outfit, exuding all the colour and confidence in the world. I'm wearing my hot-pink, Barbie-branded bum bag, a red-and-white-checked ruffled top and shorts set, a big straw hat with an oversized bow, and a smile that could melt an iceberg. If this girl could see me now, I think she'd be proud.

Growing up, I went through various phases of what I wanted to do – including becoming an actor, a fashion designer, a journalist and at one stage a forensic psychologist. But I think, deep down, I always knew I was going to end up working somewhere in business. I had that hunger in me. I just don't think I realised I'd wade through a sea of grey before coming back to myself in full colour.

Coming into this project of writing my first book, I had a fairly high level of confidence. I'd written for years previously through my blog and spoken about many of the topics I'd be discussing in this book through my podcast, or in workshops, keynotes and coaching.

I was so wrong. This book has been a roller-coaster ride – of the very best kind.

Writing this book forced me to dig right into my core, and to challenge myself and the things I say I stand for. I needed to look at myself in the mirror and ask if I was prepared to continue to stand by them on paper for the world to see. In writing this book, I was also forced to expose the vulnerable side of me, but balance it with the competent and capable side.

Truth be told, I struggled to balance these things in the early years of my career. For too long I leant too far into thinking I needed to *look* competent, to the exclusion of being who I was – a human *being* first and foremost. I squashed the part of me that made me *me*.

What a waste to think that humans create spaces where we hold back the very best parts of ourselves to fit into a box we think we have to in order to succeed. For so long I thought I had to fit into one of these boxes, and realistically, when I looked around me, it's no wonder why. The messages I was receiving about what it took to get ahead in your career were to work really, *really* hard, say you're busy all the time and take yourself way too seriously. I'd been dragged into a world of grey blazers, jargon, acronyms and fake smiles, and then I tried to fit into that mould, thinking that would get me ahead and make me happy.

I'm here to tell you that it didn't, and it doesn't – far from it, in fact. I now know that the most successful leaders are those who have taken the baggage of who they think they *need* to be off their backs. These leaders own and are accountable to who they are, what they bring and the value that they add with confidence and conviction. Surprisingly, the world becomes easier and more enjoyable – *and* you achieve more – when you choose to take the armour off. You win. Your team wins. Your organisation wins.

Writing this book has only further solidified for me that the *human* element of me is what has made me successful – my heart, humour, grit, vulnerability and perseverance. My *human-ness*. My knowledge, skills and expertise are what I do, not what's gotten me to where I am.

That is what this book is about. *Less Hustle, More Happy* helps you tap back into what makes you *you*, and more importantly, what it is you want to get out of your roughly 25,550 days on planet Earth (if you live to the global average of 70), and how you want to show up for yourself. If you're ready to take your enthusiasm, effort and expertise and turn it into something that gets results *and* feels good at the same time, this book is for you.

When people ask me what I do, I tell them three things:

1. I help organisations keep their best talent by supporting them to create an environment where people can thrive.

2. I help individuals *be* the best talent that everyone wants in their teams.

3. I speak to leaders daily about what it would mean for them to lead themselves in a way that they can feel proud of *and* still get results.

This book is designed for early- and mid-career professionals, and emerging leaders who have been taught that being the hardest worker is the *only* way to get ahead, often at the cost of being happy. This book will help you understand how you can do both – get ahead at work and avoid selling your soul while doing it.

Lastly, this book is for that little girl in her checked two-piece and straw hat, and to tell her, 'Hey, we did it, and we did it by owning who we are'.

Buckle up.

Introduction

Why do we need another career book?

We are in a disengagement epidemic, and it's costing us all considerably. (Yes, Houston, we have a problem.) Gallup's *State of the Global Workplace: 2024 Report* highlights that low engagement is estimated to be costing the global economy $8.9 trillion per year through lost productivity, absenteeism and turnover.

You read that correctly – $8.9 trillion, which, at the time of writing, is 9 per cent of global GDP. And according to Gallup CEO Jon Clifton, that amount is enough to make the difference between success and a failure for humanity. Clifton goes on to argue:

> *Gallup's research into wellbeing at work finds that having a job you hate is worse than being unemployed – and those negative emotions end up at home, impacting relationships with family. If you're not thriving at work, you're unlikely to be thriving at life.*

I couldn't agree more with this.

The old ways aren't working anymore. You've changed, I've changed – we've all changed. And yet, even post-pandemic, the working world is largely still structured based on ways of the past.

A world where 'enough' doesn't exist

We operate in a world that seems to want us to have more, do more, be more and own more, even though many of us mere mortals are now asking, 'There must be more to life, right?'

We now have five generations in the workforce, all with different experiences, worldviews, opinions, values and ways of doing things. And they're all colliding. That's five different generations of humans navigating a landscape we know we've outgrown, yet it still has its arms tightly wrapped around us like an octopus refusing to release its prey.

What you don't need is another career book telling you how to hustle, or squeeze even more juice out of your already overflowing day. What you also don't need is another book telling your manager how to lead. Books that focus on these topics are critical, and I have many of them on my bookshelf, but often something is missing from a leading *self* perspective – a perspective that enables you as an individual to lead yourself forward in a way you can take pride in, and in a way your team and organisation can also be proud of.

You don't need to wait until you formally 'become a leader' to lead. You lead in the way you achieve outcomes with other humans, and by leading a life that leaves things better than you found them.

More human BEING, less human DOING

This book will help you get back to the fundamentals of what it means to actually be a human *being*, instead of just a human *doing*, living a life with connection, fulfilment, vulnerability, heart and humour, self-determination and intentionality. Ultimately, this book will help you channel your expertise, effort and enthusiasm in a direction that not only sees results for your team and organisation but also feels good along the way.

Do you ever feel as if you've got one foot firmly planted on the accelerator and your handbrake pulled at the same time? Do you feel like you're at full throttle but going nowhere? Or, if you are going somewhere, you're not sure whether it's somewhere you want to be going? Things have become stuck and stale – including in the way we approach our careers and each other, and often even in the way our employers are trying to motivate us. We're pushing so hard, but we've lost sight of why and whether the pushing is moving us forward or just creating a community of burnt-out zombies wandering around in the pursuit of 'more'.

For all the technological advancements we've made over the years, it feels as though we are more stressed, exhausted and dis-connected than ever before. The goal posts have shifted and will continue to, which means we need to step back into the driver's seat and redefine success on our terms. Think that's not possible? I don't blame you. Everything around you is telling you to just work harder, push through and take on more responsibilities, and that that is the only way you'll get ahead.

With over 16 years in human resources roles across multiple different industries and countries, however, I have seen a thing or two (or three!) about what differentiates those who get what they want at work, have the impact they intend to *and* enjoy the journey, versus those who, well, don't.

***Spoiler alert*: What makes a star employee isn't what you think.**

What's interesting about the thousands of conversations that I've had with leaders over the years about what they value the most in their star employees is that, more often than not, it doesn't come down to the hardest worker, or even the most technically astute person. Instead, it is a unique set of behaviours and traits that, when intentionally and consistently leveraged, equal an employee who is seen, valued and developed beyond their wildest dreams. I outline this unique set of behaviours and practices throughout this book, and adopting and consistently acting on them will see you leading a happy career, not just one of hustle.

I've also included Your Happy Career Action boxes in the following chapters, which include questions for you to reflect on, activities to complete, and actions designed to help you put into practice what you are learning. You can also scan the QR code at the back of the book to gain access to me on a deeper level, as well as more exclusive resources to help you continue to learn and grow.

My sincere hope is that by the end of this book you will have received enough of a loving nudge to ask yourself the hard questions and implement some changes that, if you stick to them, will see you having both a career you can feel proud of and a life in accordance with your definition of success.

I know you're going out on a limb trusting me here. But one thing I can absolutely guarantee you is this: if you don't *choose* to change, nothing will change. It's time to stop the unhelpful career habits that have seen you stuck, unfulfilled and hustling for far too long.

It's time to focus again on happy.

Chapter 1

Working harder is no longer enough

Within the overall aim of introducing more happy and less hustle at work, let's first talk about the idea of 'hustle culture' and 'busyness' – and why simply working harder is not the answer. Does the following sound familiar?

'Hey, Sally. How are you?'

'Soooooooooo busy. It's crazy right now, isn't it?'

'Oh, I know, me too. I've been working every night this week, and on weekends. It's just hectic.'

'Me too. It's just so busy at the moment. I need more hours in the day. Bring on the weekend.'

A dialogue similar to this is happening in most organisations around Australia most days.

Here is something I've observed inside organisations over the years, though. We often convince ourselves that we work really, really hard – like, seriously hard. And we often use the metrics of inputs and the symptoms of those inputs, such as stress levels, to measure our contribution. (I talk more about the language of business and inputs in chapter 6.) And yet, in reality, when we break it down, we find we aren't efficient. We aren't effective. And we aren't delivering to our full potential.

You might disagree. You might have convinced yourself of the benefits of being busy, but my question is this: are you busy with the *right* things? Are you busy with the things that *really matter*? Are you busy with the *priorities* of your manager or department, or the strategic and financial objectives of the organisation overall?

Or, have you busied yourself with things you think are important, but really aren't?

Getting busy in all the wrong ways

I remember once spending days on a PowerPoint presentation to outline for my senior leadership team our HR strategy for the year ahead. I'm talking *days*. It was beautiful – it looked sleek and had all the usual buzzwords a strategy document should include, such as 'competitive advantage', 'leading and lagging indicators', 'scorecard' and, of course, my favourite, 'performance drivers'.

Do you know what happened when I shared my presentation in that leadership team meeting? The first question I got from my fellow leaders was, 'How are you going to implement all of that?' The second was, 'Why are these considered the priorities when we've got all these other changes happening?' Gulp. Dear world, please swallow me whole immediately.

I'd made two critical errors. Firstly, I'd spent far too long doing something that made *me* feel busy and accomplished but wasn't actually important to my core stakeholders. Secondly, and probably worse than the first, I hadn't had the right relationship conversations and hadn't flexed my social awareness muscle (also known as understanding the office politics at play) ahead of this meeting to know what was important to the people in my orbit, and then communicated it to them in a way that ensured they felt seen, heard and involved.

I delve into the factors behind the second mistake in far more detail in chapters 5 and 6 of this book, where I look at the importance of relationships in building a successful career, and performance currency. My first mistake, however, was more about my own comfort, my own ego, and prioritising what I considered necessary to look accomplished and satisfy my own inner critic over the needs of the organisation.

Now, don't get me wrong, I'm not saying that strategy doesn't matter. It absolutely does. What I am saying is that your ability to read the tone of your team and your organisation and be able to anticipate what is truly important to them at any point in time are critical skills to master if you want less hustle and more happy in your career.

In the following chapters, I help you target your efforts, expertise and enthusiasm in ways that are meaningful and lead to outcomes that your stakeholders *actually* care about – in turn, helping you do your work with greater ease and enjoyment.

Effort, expertise and enthusiasm: the trifecta

Having worked with thousands of people over the years across different industries, countries, demographics and cultures, I've been able to observe and reflect on what makes a career built more on happy and less on hustle.

I sum it up in this formula:

Targeted effort + meaningful contribution of expertise + enthusiasm = happy career

A happy career sees you channelling your efforts and contributing your expertise (knowledge, skills and talents) in a way that feels meaningful and is fuelled by enthusiasm.

Here's what it looks like when you are operating from a place of highly targeted *effort*:

· You know what 'great' looks like, and you have clarity around outcomes needed.

· You know who to engage and how to engage them – you have a targeted approach.

· You're responsive instead of reactive, because you have the discipline to zoom out and assess the bigger picture of your priorities.

· You get meaningful sh*t done, instead of just shallow work that wears you down over time.

And when you're operating from a place of high *enthusiasm*, it looks like this:

· You're intrinsically motivated.

· You know what your career values are and you live them daily through your actions.

· You know your own value and you utilise your strengths regularly and deliberately.

· You have an attitude of optimism and resilience.

· You operate from a growth-oriented mindset.

Your *expertise* is the skills, knowledge and talents that you bring to your role. The more aware you are of these, and the more deliberately you utilise them, the more this contributes to both your targeted efforts and your enthusiasm.

Finding your happy place

When it comes to the combination of effort and enthusiasm, I've identified that most people sit in one of the four quadrants of my Happy Career Matrix, shown in figure 1.

Figure 1: Happy Career Matrix

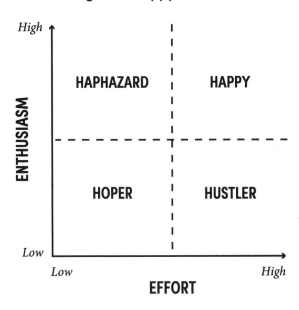

Without the intentionality that sits behind building a career of happy, you can easily end up in one of the other three quadrants. Every one of these quadrants has ramifications for you, your team and your organisation.

Here are the characteristics of each of the four quadrants:

- **The Hoper** *(low effort, low enthusiasm)*. You sit back waiting to be told by your manager what your development plan is, what training or development will be provided to you, or what your next career step will be. You show up and you tick your job 'boxes', but you aren't really putting yourself out there for opportunities, or proactively seeking to be a team player and demonstrate your potential. You are waiting, hoping that someone will see what you're capable of and 'gift' you an opportunity that you might be open to.

- **The Hustler** *(high effort, low enthusiasm)*. You are often running from meeting to meeting and task to task, and probably putting in some serious hours. Despite your inputs, though (long hours, energy and stress), you aren't getting the rewards you're hoping for. Perhaps you're not feeling like your work is overly meaningful, you're not creating the impact you really want, or you're struggling to get results from your efforts. You often get to the end of your day, breathe out a big sigh and think, *There must be another way*.

- **The Haphazard** *(low effort, high enthusiasm)*. You bring bursts of optimism, energy and enthusiasm for yourself and your team. But it isn't consistent, and it's not targeted. You've got all the ingredients to make it happen, except the part to actually make it happen! Your enthusiasm is great, but it just doesn't seem to translate to you getting meaningful outcomes from your skills and expertise. You're bringing the right attitude, but not the targeted action and efforts that are needed to get results.

- **The Happy** *(high effort, high enthusiasm)*. You're self-motivated and clear on what your definition of success is, as well as how you can get yourself, your team and your organisation there. You are clear on how your resources (time, expertise and effort) translate to high-impact outcomes that are meaningful, and you motivate others along the way. You're clear on your career values and your personal 'why', which means you're able to withstand almost any 'how'. You're resilient, optimistic and open to change and feedback.

So, where do you sit on my Happy Career Matrix? Over to you.

Your Happy Career Action

Reflect on the Happy Career Matrix shown in the preceding figure, and read through the explanations just provided for each one of the four quadrants. Where do you currently see yourself, and why?

The sunk-cost effect

Claire, your grades are showing that your strongest subjects at the moment are accounting and drama, so you might want to look at university pathways in accounting and finance because they are fairly safe career options for you.

I remember this conversation with the careers counsellor at my school when I was preparing to enter year 11. I was 15 years old at the time. The irony of accounting and drama being my two strongest subjects is not lost on me, but what stays with me the most is the gentle (*read: strong*) nudging and influencing even at that age to direct me into a 'safe' career purely based on what I was good at. At no point was I ever asked which subjects I liked, or what I enjoyed doing.

Fast-forward a few years and I did go on to university to study accounting and finance, but after 12 months I wanted to gouge my eyes out with forks (sorry to all my finance friends!) and ended up switching to marketing, management and human resources. Was this a better decision? Who knows?! What I do know, though, is that I'm now operating in a space with more fun and fulfilling days than ever before.

I think many people have had a similar experience to mine. We enter career pathways based on what we were told we were good at in school. And when I say 'what we were told we were good at', I mean the things we got good *(ish)* grades in, or that were considered safe and stable pathways we could climb the ladder in. Seldom were we invited to step back and think about what we actually enjoyed doing. My careers counsellor didn't ask what put me into a state of flow, where time just seemed to pass by in an instant, or what filled my cup. I also wasn't asked what kinds of activities or subjects give me energy, or what I was passionate about that the world actually needed.

No, for many of us, the focus was just on identifying what you are good at, and then working out how you could use that to pay your bills for the next 50 years. Around 15 years after making these decisions at such a young age, however, people will often approach me saying they feel unfulfilled, stuck and in a career that absolutely does not light them up. I am not surprised.

Even though they may feel stuck in their careers, people still often struggle to make a change, in part due to the sunk-cost effect. Christopher Olivola, an assistant professor of marketing at Carnegie Mellon's Tepper School of Business and author of 'The interpersonal sunk-cost effect' (published in the journal *Psychological Science*), defines the sunk-cost effect as the general tendency for people to continue an endeavour, or continue consuming or pursuing an option, if they've invested time or money or some other resource in it. Olivola argues that effect 'becomes a fallacy if it's pushing you to do things that are making you unhappy or worse off'. This can be true for the hobbies we invest money into, the courses we take, the college or university degrees we complete, the relationships we're in and, of course, the jobs and career pathways we invest into. The more we've invested, the harder it often becomes to leave.

As an example of this, Eva recently contacted me looking for one-on-one coaching support. When we jumped on the call together and I asked her what prompted her to reach out, she said,

'I feel stuck and in a rut in my career, but I feel like I've come so far now that I just have to suck it up'. Eva was 37. We then went on to have a conversation about what her definition of career success was and what she would need to do for herself to feel proud in another 15 years' time.

Eva had never considered what it was that *she* valued in her career, or what impact *she* wanted to have and what contribution *she* wanted to make. Following some reflection around this, Eva left our session feeling more empowered and in control, and clear on her values and definition of success. She was ready to make a career transition, feeling confident that staying in the role she was currently in just because she had been there for so long wasn't a good enough reason.

On average, we're living longer – which often means we're working longer. Given the increasing cost of living, ongoing changes to the pension accessibility age (in Australia), and a longer life expectancy, many of us will be working until we are about 70.

A National Seniors Australia report from 2022 found that of some 3000 retirees surveyed, 17.3 per cent had re-entered the workforce since retiring, and a further 18.5 per cent were considering it. The primary reason? To earn more money. A number of respondents explicitly cited financial stress and not being able to live off the age pension as their key motivators.

Notwithstanding the very real economic challenges and cost of living crisis that we are facing as a society, are you really going to lock yourself in with perhaps 30-plus years left on the working timer and say that you are too far in to make a career change? I really hope not. And yet, the sunk-cost effect keeps so many people doing just that – stuck in jobs or careers they hate, hustling away, and counting down the days until they retire (if they are lucky enough to live to retirement). They are not living a career or a life that is built on happy.

Find your purpose, find your happy

Japan's Okinawa Island is considered to be one of the world's five 'blue zones', with a very high concentration of centenarians. In 2015, the number of centenarians living in Okinawa per 100,000 people was double the number living in the rest of Japan.

Fast-forward to 2021, and according to its health ministry Japan's centenarian population overall hit a record high of 86,510 people, an increase of 6060 from 2020 – and up from just 153 when records began in 1963. This means that one Japanese person in every 1450 is now aged over 100. Women account for 88.4 per cent of centenarians, with the people of Okinawa still making up the biggest portion of centenarians.

Many of the people of Okinawa attribute their long lives to something called *ikigai*. Sadly, and this is possibly representative of western culture, the English language doesn't have a direct translation for *ikigai*. However, it can be loosely translated to 'reason for being', 'meaning in life' or 'happiness in living', and why we do what we do.

Delving deeper into the concept of *ikigai* allows you to see that purpose or meaning can be found in the intersection of four key areas:

1. what you love
2. what you are good at
3. what you believe the world needs
4. what you can live off.

Where people often go wrong is thinking that this 'meaning' is only acquired through their nine-to-five jobs. The risk you run with this kind of pressure is tying up too much of your identity with your career. Insert a work redundancy, a restructure, a significant life event or something else that takes you out of the workforce for a while, and all of a sudden you can feel like you've lost who you are. You can feel you no longer have a strong purpose or meaning. You can allow your identity to be so tied up in a job that you forget it's only a part of who you are, not ALL that you are.

Ikigai is about finding meaning and value in life, and we can do this by reflecting on our contribution in life – any kind of contribution.

The best part is that the more meaning we can find through different kinds of contribution, the better and more enthusiastic we will likely become at our paid work, because it's just one part of what makes life valuable.

Is this an existential crisis?

In their book *Ikigai: The Japanese secret to a long and happy life*, researchers Hector García and Francesc Miralles talk about existential frustration versus existential crisis. They argue existential frustration 'arises when our life is without purpose, or when that purpose is skewed', whereas existential crisis comes about in modern societies when people 'do what they are told to do, or what others do, rather than what they want to do'. According to García and Miralles, in the latter situation people typically try to fill the gap between these expectations and what they really want for themselves with 'economic power or physical pleasure, or by numbing their senses'. While a crisis cuts deeper, existential frustration can actually be a positive thing and what García and Miralles call 'a catalyst for change'.

They go on to expand on German philosopher Friedrich Nietzsche's idea that 'He who has a why to live for can bear almost any how'. Essentially, when you know why you do what you do, and what truly matters to you, the bad days, the setbacks and the inconveniences of life don't bother you as much.

Perhaps what you need, then, instead of blindly following a career based on a one-dimensional view of success, is to accept that career success is not about perfection or promotion, but about how can you strive for a life that sees you contributing by utilising your skills, talents and passions in ways that stretch and challenge you, and feel meaningful.

Finding meaning at work

Organisational psychology specialist Professor Adam Grant surmises that what motivates employees is 'doing work that affects the wellbeing of others' and to 'see or meet the people affected by their work'.

Even outside some of the obvious career pathways devoted to caring for others, such as nursing, teaching and psychology, and irrespective of your role, you can still be more deliberate about understanding the impact of your work on others. However, zooming out and asking yourself bigger questions around *what* impact you want to have and what makes you feel good requires conscious effort.

I saw a sign in a store recently that just said this: 'Choose your hard'. It has stayed with me since. Spending time getting clear on who you are and what you really value is *hard*. Continuing blindly in life feeling unfulfilled and not finding things that bring you joy is *hard*. Stepping back and looking at your career and the areas you can grow, unlearn and relearn is *hard*. Rocking up to work every day saying you're overwhelmed and too busy to invest in your growth is *hard*.

Choose your hard.

A dissatisfied human equals a dissatisfied employee

When you aren't happy at your core, or feel you aren't utilising your talents, skills, passions or potential, or are unable to find some sort of meaning in your work, you can often become disgruntled, resentful or frustrated. And you usually become somebody that most people don't want to work with. This dissatisfaction can then translate into how you lead yourself at work, lead your team, collaborate with peers and lead for organisational outcomes.

Deep in your core, you know when you've lost sight of your definition of success. Or, maybe you never created one to start with.

The people have spoken

In my work as a career and leadership trainer and coach, one of my favourite things to do when working with new groups of people is to get a flavour for what they feel their biggest career and leadership challenges currently are. This not only gives me a sense of the key themes at play inside the organisation, it also provides helpful insights into which bits of my expertise to share to help them navigate these challenges for greater career resilience and, ultimately, deliver better outcomes for their organisation.

No matter what company I go to, the same core desires consistently prevail. They might be worded slightly differently, but they almost always come back to this: **Human beings at their core want to feel heard, seen, valued and understood.**

Sounds simple, right? Obvious, even. Yet, time and time again the biggest challenges you likely face or the biggest frustrations you hold are caused by feeling someone hasn't done this for you.

Here is just a micro snippet of what workshop participants have shouted out to me when I ask about their career challenges and what they feel they need:

- 'Better emotional management and ability to deal with overwhelm. Managing people and complex people/problems daily has left me feeling exhausted.'

- 'Doing work that I feel is actually making a difference.'
- 'Building a broader network and a stronger ability to influence people and showcase value without feeling arrogant.'
- 'Deeper clarity on my own impact and the value that I can add to my manager and team.'
- 'How to successfully influence stakeholders when everyone seems to have their own agenda.'
- 'Feeling inspired again by my career and the opportunities that are out there after returning to the workforce after having children.'
- 'Being more strategic about the relationships I have and consistently building my own network, instead of just focusing on my immediate tasks.'
- 'Switching off and setting boundaries – being able to say no and feel like that is okay.'
- 'Managing competing agendas, limited time and seemingly endless deliverables that everyone wanted yesterday.'
- 'Knowing my strengths and being confident to use them more often.'
- 'Feeling okay to break career ladder norms and do what I want to do without feeling guilty.'

Do any of these resonate with you? Do you see these play out in your workplace?

You're not alone if you're feeling any of these things, but my advice to you is this: **Hope is *not* a strategy.**

Waiting and hoping that your organisation will take care of this for you, or that these challenges will go away, is not enough. You have got to get out in front of them too. You have got to lead yourself first.

What's your career currency?

At the time of writing, a simple Google search of the phrase 'What is success?' provided me with 9,430,000,000 options, all with certain aspects in common. According to *Cambridge Dictionary*, success is 'The achieving of results wanted or hoped for', while *Collins Dictionary* defines it as 'The achievement of something that you have been trying to do'. However, the definition that I think is truly representative of what society expects of us comes from *Encyclopaedia Britannica*: 'the fact of getting or achieving wealth, respect, or fame'.

Here's what grinds my gears when I read these, though. All these definitions of success are an end state. They all rely on the thing we *think* we want happening in order for us to finally declare ourselves successful or happy. What about the journey along the way? Are we completely discounting the way in which we get to the finish line? And what happens after we are 'successful'? Do we just stop? Retire? Die? And, what happens if what we deem to be success changes along the way? Does that mean we failed?

I want to talk about a career where you can be successful on your terms *and* still support your organisation.

You can have a career story where you believe you are also successful *along* the journey, and not just upon the accomplishment of whatever big, shiny thing might be calling you at the top of the ladder. You can define a career where you are intentional about the ways you can enjoy it, and where success is based more on the enjoyment of the whole journey and less about ticking the box at the very end. This is a happy career.

I remember thinking I had the career success formula absolutely nailed. Do the longest hours. Be the hardest worker. Say yes to everything. Success will *hopefully* follow. It would be remiss of me not to admit that some truth exists in this approach, and that this one-dimensional formula afforded me some success in the earlier stages of my career. However, I have long since recognised that this strategy was never going to get me into roles of influence inside an organisation, or help me build a sustainable career based on happy, not on hustle.

I'm going to swing for the fences here and make a bold statement in contradiction to the previous definitions of success, and that is that you are *already* successful. You wouldn't be reading this right now if you weren't. Chances are, however, you've been able to achieve this success by doing one or more of the following:

- work really, really hard
- regularly take on more and more tasks, even when you don't have capacity to
- say yes to everything (and probably resent it later)
- be a 'solid contributor' who's always prepared to go above and beyond to get things done
- ultimately, deliver more than what is asked.

Fair assumption?

Perhaps you hope that by doing all this someone in a position of power or influence will eventually notice, and all of your hard work and sacrifices will be rewarded in the manner of a promotion, a pay rise or whatever career opportunity you hope will edge you closer to that elusive 'success'.

But let me remind you of something.

Louder for those at the back: hope is *not* a career strategy.

Hustle is also not a strong strategy. In fact, eventually it can be the thing that derails us, because we become miserable, unmotivated, burnt out and resentful – towards ourselves and our colleagues or organisations.

Organisations need more than just your inputs. They need you to be able to take *what* you know, work effectively with *who* you know, and act upon it with others in a way that drives growth and delivers on financial and strategic outcomes.

This is where the requirement of a strong career currency comes in. Coined by Carla Harris, Vice Chairman and Senior Client Advisor at Morgan Stanley, this concept highlights that two very powerful currencies are at play in organisations: relationship and performance. As shown in figure 2, you need to consistently hold solid currency in both.

Figure 2: Career currency

Here's how the two currencies work together:

- **Relationship currency** is determined by the way you achieve outcomes through the relationships you have and the influence you hold in your company. Who do you know, who do you need to know you, and how effective are your relationships with them? What influence do you have?

· **Performance currency** is determined by the way in which you demonstrate what you know, and deliver on the things you're accountable for and more. Your key stakeholders assume you are able to do your job, but for you to really elevate the worth of your performance currency, they need to see your ability to demonstrate your potential. Note again, my friends, this isn't just about hustling harder.

Where you can go wrong is to only focus on the performance part. You work super hard and hope someone will notice. However, what actually drives a career that sees you becoming the blue-chip stock everyone wants to invest in for the long term is a combination of both your relationships and your performance. That combination is what strengthens your career currency.

At this point, you might be wondering, *How do both things lead to a happier me? They just sound like more work.* Don't worry, I've got you covered.

What you're going to do over the coming pages is unlearn years of habits and replace them with new, actionable strategies to move you forward in a way that feels good *and* sees results. This is where my five-part career framework comes into play, my friend.

A happy career is built on five elements

In addition to relationship and performance currency, three more considerations help you take your career from hustling to happy. Figure 3 shows the elements of my five-part career framework, and in chapters 3 to 7 I dive into each one of these elements in a way that empowers you to take action for yourself and take the steps towards a sustainable career built on happy.

Figure 3: My five-part career framework

Here's a rundown of the five elements of a happy career.

Element one: Knowing yourself and setting your vision

What do you know about yourself? Who are you without your job? And how do you define success on your terms?

Woooooaaaahhh. Calm your farm, Claire, you might be thinking. *I just want you to tell me how to be happy.* I know – we've started strong, haven't we?

In element one, covered in chapter 3, I help you dive deep into why self-awareness is your number-one career superpower. I look at the power of mindset and understanding your own career beliefs, and identifying your inner critic. I help you get specific about your personal definition of career success and your career values. My hope is that by the end of the chapter you'll feel empowered by the knowledge that success isn't just an end-state but also a journey to be enjoyed that looks different for everyone.

Element two: Cultivating your bold brand

Have you ever considered how you want to be perceived in your organisation? How would you like people to describe you when you're not in the room? Consider your team, your manager, your peers and colleagues – what would you hope that they would say about you?

Getting clear and intentional on what you want your professional brand to look like, and then consistently demonstrating behaviours to go with that, is critical to cultivating a reliable and credible brand authentic to you. In chapter 4, I ask you to reflect on your own reputation at work and craft a unique selling proposition (USP) aligned with your strengths and superpowers.

Element three: Accelerating growth through relationships

You can rapidly accelerate your impact inside an organisation through a focus on building and nurturing real, genuine and effective working relationships. However, you may often find yourself prioritising the task, process or project over the people.

What does it mean to invest in relationships consistently and authentically? I help you dig into this and more in chapter 5, as well as looking at the different types of networks you need to foster for your long-term career, and why influence is the new power supply in business.

Element four: Building your performance currency

Yes, you need to be good at your job; however, as I hope you're starting to realise, just working harder and hoping you'll get to where you want to go isn't a strong plan conducive to a happy and sustainable career. What are the outcomes of the work that you do? How do they serve the strategic or financial objectives of your organisation? And how do you speak the language of the business to increase your own performance currency? *Psst... I promise you, this isn't as scary as it might sound.*

I also outline the other necessary skills you need to develop to increase your performance currency, including the way you navigate conflict and feedback, strategically self-promote *and* communicate effectively.

Element five: Future-proofing yourself!

To round out the five elements, in chapter 7 I outline the tools you need to stay relevant at work. No doubt you know the world is moving at a rapid pace, and it isn't showing signs of slowing down any time soon. Therefore, it is important that you continue to find ways to stay relevant and ahead of the change curve.

To do this well and consistently, you need to not just strengthen your career resilience cardio but also pump some anti-fragility weights. You need to learn to get comfortable with change and setbacks in all forms, because I guarantee you, there will be some. Your aim is to set yourself up for a future where you feel confident and comfortable to ask for things you want, so in chapter 7 I also look at how you can continue to negotiate for yourself and get what you want at work.

This ain't no #bosslife cocktails by the pool party, though.

It is probably important at this point to let you know that this book will not teach you how to sit by the pool with a cocktail and your laptop, working for one hour a day and calling it #bosslife or #millionairemindset. This book isn't a leadership development guide teaching you how to drive high-performing teams, either – although, if you do lead a team, you can benefit immensely from sharing this book with them and (hopefully) creating an army of enthusiastic, engaged employees.

What this book can help you with is harnessing your efforts and expertise in a way that will get you better outcomes and get you closer to *your* definition of career success – and cause your enthusiasm to skyrocket in the process. This book will teach you how to *be* a high-performing, high-impact employee for yourself in a way that is motivating and sustainable. It can also enable you to position yourself as an 'in-demand' employee who everyone wants on their team. This provides you with options, and options are a key ingredient of a career built on happy.

So, my friend, what do you think?

Are you ready to open your mind to a new way of working? One that sees you adopt targeted strategies that leverage your strengths and increase your career currency in a way that will open more doors than you ever imagined? More importantly, are you ready to do the work? This is not an easy read. I don't want you to think, *That was interesting*, and then shove this book back on your shelf to collect dust while you change nothing.

My hope is that you'll dig into this book and put the provided tools into practice in your own life, because that's the only way you'll move from hustle to happy.

Remember: *choose your hard*.

Let's do it!

Your Happy Career Action

Reflect on your own career. What feels good right now? What feels challenging or difficult? If failure wasn't an option, how would you solve the challenges? What conversations would you need to have? Now, what is one small step forward you can take to get the ball moving for yourself?

Momentum breeds momentum, and action builds confidence.

Chapter 2

Career lessons, learnings and expert insights

Truth be told, I've made some CLMs (career-limiting moves) in my time.

There was the time I hit my CFO in the head with a pool cue after getting a little too excited.

Or the time I spotted a senior leader who I thought looked like he needed an escape route from a conversation he was stuck in. I went up to him and casually said under my breath, 'I'm here to save you from this conversation' – and he then responded by introducing me to his wife.

Or that time I wrote an email with the subject header 'Is the monster gone yet?' with reference to my boss at the time. I then sent it to my boss. Gulp.

Maybe some of these are familiar to you? Perhaps you have your own CLM stories? Funny as these may be, though, they still aren't as critical as the real CLMs that I share in this chapter. And don't worry – I also introduce some ways to break out of these career traps.

A personal insight into career lessons and traps

I recall stepping into my first senior role within an organisation right when it was going through an incredible amount of change. I felt out of my depth and like a total imposter, and I went to work most days waiting for the tap on the shoulder from my boss telling me, 'Thanks, Claire, but no thanks'. I lay awake most nights criticising myself for the things I'd said (or hadn't said) that day, thinking that surely people would be judging and laughing, and questioning my credibility and competence. I thought most must be wondering why on earth I was in this role.

To compensate for these insecurities, I worked – more and more and more. I stopped making time for myself completely, and I most certainly stopped believing in myself and my own abilities. I was operating in an almost constant state of panic and overwhelm, and the stories I was telling myself were absolutely the result of a fixed mindset. If I didn't know it already, I thought, I never could.

I had gotten to the stage where I really believed I couldn't do it. I felt like a total failure, and I started questioning other parts of my life too. For a person who generally takes a 'glass half full' approach to life, it was a really lonely and sad place to be. I was in my own head, drowning in my own thoughts.

There has to be more to work (and life) than hustling

I was definitely hustling and not at all happy. 'This can't be it, surely', I'd often say to myself before closing my eyes at night after another long, soul-destroying day.

But, here's the thing. I didn't ask for help. I didn't ask for feed-back. I didn't look up or look around. Instead, I let the internal noise cave in on me. I let my negative mindset and my self-limiting career beliefs get the better of me, and then I just worked harder to avoid having to deal with them. In addition to adopting a fixed mindset – where I believed I was either totally competent or a total failure – I had also taken a really short-term view of my career. Likely, this was because I'd become so consumed by my own feelings that I couldn't see the forest for the trees.

As I look back now, I can see just how important it is to take a long-term and holistic view of your career. Just as your mind and body need to be nurtured and nourished, so too does your career if you want it to last – and thrive.

A manifesto of career lessons for the long game

If I could go back and enlighten myself with what I know now about the true ingredients of a long-term, sustainable career, these are the points I would run through:

1. Working harder and longer hours and just hoping someone will notice is *not* the answer. Look up, and look around you. The people who get the opportunities are usually the people who build sincere relationships and then go and ask for those opportunities.

2. Selling yourself and your potential is not an option, it is a necessity. The project you've just brought to life that is making your team 30 per cent more efficient might be fabulous, but if no-one knows about it because you are too worried about sounding 'braggy', you'll miss out on opportunities. P.S. I can assure you – the people who are worried about sounding braggy are never the ones who actually are.

3. In order to sell yourself, you must know the value you add. This means you must know yourself well enough to know your strengths and weaknesses. And while I'm on strengths, knowing your strengths alone is not enough. You must own

them and be competent in leveraging them consistently for business outcomes.

4. I hate to break this to you, but it is not your manager's job to guess what your aspirations are. It is your job to tell them, regularly and gracefully, and then find ways to proactively upskill yourself to get yourself to where you want to go. Passively waiting for your manager to give you a development plan, or only choosing to invest in yourself if your company will foot the bill, are sure-fire ways to become irrelevant.

5. Your perception is your projection, just as the next person's is theirs. Be aware of what you tell yourself, because it isn't always the truth.

6. If you want to be seen as a truly credible and competent high-flyer in your company, you must speak the language of the business. Even more importantly, you need to remember that your reputation and brand is built in the micro-moments, not just in the one-off sweeping gestures.

7. Constantly being the person to shrink so that others can rise will hurt you in the long run, but repeatedly alienating others won't help you either. Balance is key. You need to speak to be heard and listen to understand.

8. Just because you communicated something doesn't mean your message was heard. Effective communication is when you deliver a message, it is received the way you wanted it to be *and* the right action has been taken based on the way it was understood. Learn this now – most people will do only the first part of effective communication for their entire careers, and then claim that no-one ever listened to them.

9. Build, nurture and leverage your networks and relationships through your whole career, *not* just when you need something.

Do it with sincere intent. Regularly being the last one in the office when others are out making new connections and building relationships will not serve you in the long run. As introduced in chapter 1, a strong career currency is made up of performance currency *and* relationship currency.

10. You *will* get feedback that you don't like throughout your career. Learn to get comfortable with it and remain curious. Enhance your capacity to give and receive feedback. The ability to engage in mature and meaningful feedback conversations, and then close the loop on feedback that you receive, will be one of the single best skills you can learn to be seen as a high-potential employee and self-aware leader.

These are the lessons I've learnt (often the hard way), and I expand on them through the rest of this book. Taking these lessons and learnings into consideration for yourself is important when it comes to building a sustainable career more on happy and less on hustle. Before we delve any further, however, let's also hear from other experts on what they value in high-performing, high-impact employees.

What really makes a 'star' employee?

Perhaps you've said similar statements to the following, or asked similar questions:

- 'I want to be seen as a high performer.'
- 'I want to be considered a high-potential employee inside my organisation.'
- 'I want more opportunities.'
- 'How can I make a bigger impact?'
- 'How can I be seen as "ready" for that next step?'

Have you been curious about finding out some of the answers for yourself? Perhaps you've wondered about the conversations that happen behind closed doors that determine who gets promoted – and, more importantly, how you can demonstrate your own potential.

It's one thing for me to share my lived experiences from countless conversations with CEOs, CFOs and managers on the employees who get ahead and those that don't, but I think what will really serve you is hearing multiple insights from talent experts who are also in the game right now in some of Australia's biggest or most well known businesses and brands.

Play the long game: a conversation with Andrea Chapman

Andrea Chapman is Executive General Manager of People for Mineral Resources Limited, a top-50 ASX-listed organisation and one of Australia's fastest growing resources companies, with well over 8000 employees. A huge portion of the company's growth has occurred in the last two years.

Andrea has a strong background in supporting organisations through considerable growth periods, so I wanted to understand more about what she sees as the raw ingredients and mindset required for employees to not only drive careers that light them up, but also provide benefits for organisations when they do so.

Andrea is the first to acknowledge that things cannot always be smooth sailing in fast-growing organisations, especially those that are developing and adopting cutting-edge technologies to create a better world. That is why she always encourages those around her to play the long game when it comes to their careers and the decisions they make within them:

It's easy when you have a bad day to say to yourself, 'Oh this sucks, this place is terrible and I'm not having any impact!' or to think that your progression isn't moving fast enough. However, I've really encouraged all employees at any organisation I've worked in to take the long-game mindset to their careers and how they see opportunities.

Not all growth opportunities come in a polished form or on a platter, and not all opportunities are steps up the ladder, either. Often growth comes in the areas we least expect it. We may even feel like we take a step back to then take a huge leap forward.

Zooming out and looking at what you are part of overall is a great way to remind yourself that you are making an impact and contributing, even on days when you may feel like you aren't making progress.

Asking yourself questions such as the following can help you gain perspective:

- 'Are we moving in the right direction overall?'
- 'Things may not be perfect, but are we making progress?'
- 'What can I do to keep things moving in a way that's constructive, deliberate and meaningful?'

Andrea highlights:

We live and operate in a world that moves so fast that I think we often have expectations that everything can therefore move that fast, and that everything can transform in a matter of moments. But big, transformational change does take time. It takes a targeted, collective effort, plus energy and enthusiasm, and that's why the question of 'Are we moving in the right direction?' is such a powerful one for career resilience.

When it comes to fast-moving organisations – which most organisations are these days – knowing the business you're in is critical to being able to play the long game. But what does this mean, exactly?

It means really knowing and understanding what your stakeholders care about. What concerns do they have? What challenges are they facing? Knowing how they like to receive things and how they like to communicate goes a long way to increasing your impact and influence. For example, are they detail kind of people or are they more high-level visionaries? Knowing your people, meeting them where they are at, and then speaking in a language that they can absorb is such a valued skill, but often underutilised because most of us are running around so busily with all the things we need, instead of asking the bigger questions of what our teams, stakeholders or organisations need. I think that's often where we then end up disheartened by our contribution.

That led Andrea to share one of the best pieces of guidance I have ever heard around how employees can both stay true to themselves *and* succeed inside their organisations: 'Be hungry, be humble and have heart'.

This advice is based on Patrick Lencioni's 'hungry, humble, and smart' concept for a great team player (taken from *The Ideal Team Player*). However, Andrea has adapted the concept for herself over time, based on her own experiences and human-centred approach to leading herself:

Be hungry – have a strong, intrinsic drive. Be gritty, and be able to show up with a determination and resilience to get things done, even when things feel unclear or the goalposts shift. Ask questions. Be curious. Be helpful.

Be humble – bring those around you along for the ride too. Build relationships and remember where you started. Think of others more than yourself and always be open to feedback in order to help you grow.

Have heart – be human, be vulnerable and bring your human-ness to work. You don't have to be perfect and you don't always have to have the answers. Humans want to work with humans, so connect and engage with others sincerely, and own who you are with honesty and accountability.

By remaining true to yourself and making time to 'zoom out' regularly, you will be able to see the growth and progress you are really making in your career. This will fuel your motivation to keep going and enable you to feel happier and more in control of your own development.

Defining great performance at work: a check-in with Emma Miller

Emma Miller is Head of Human Resources for APAC and Director of Global Talent for Boardriders. Having won awards for her leadership, including HR Professional of the Year at the Retail Association Awards, Emma not only talks the talk but walks it too. She's also had a front-row seat for years to the work conversations you are no doubt most curious about.

I think 99 per cent of us go to work to do a good job and perform as best we can, so I asked Emma how great performance was really measured. How can we know that what we're doing is considered good or even great by our manager?

Emma believes that defining great performance is different for different roles. However, she argues that you can do certain things to set yourself up for success and help showcase yourself as a great performer at work – and they don't require you to just work harder and lose your soul in the process.

Emma's first piece of advice is to be really consistent:

No matter what you're doing, make sure that you're consistent in the way you work. Doing something amazing once and then reverting to subpar performance or low engagement and enthusiasm in your work or with your team isn't likely to get you ahead. Consistency is key.

It's important to note, too, that consistency does *not* mean perfection. Mistakes are part of being human, but how you go about moving forward after a mistake is a key element in how your organisation views your capacity for opportunities.

Emma also recommends focusing on not just what you do but also how you do it:

It's not just about ticking off those 'to-do' lists – it's HOW you go about it that matters just as much, if not more, in the medium to long term. Do you engage multiple perspectives? Are you able to deal with setbacks or challenges along the way? It's easy to be a great employee when everything is going swimmingly, but how you navigate change, or tough times, is what really separates the good from the great.

Ever worked with a talented a**hole? You know, those people who might be technically talented (or sometimes might not even be!) and yet steamroll or alienate everyone in the process of getting results. I bet you can think of someone like that. This behaviour only gets you so far, however.

So Emma's next piece of advice is to be aware of how you are treating people along the way:

Having good technical skills isn't enough if behavioural and communication skills aren't there too. At some point in time, the business will start to realise, 'We could probably find someone who, although they may not be as technically astute, from a behavioural point of view is going to offer so much more value, and we'd rather invest in them and then support them to build their technical skills up'.

Emma knows that *how* you work with others matters. It is critical to your overall performance and to your ultimate career success. Being technically gifted but having a reputation inside the organisation as someone who is difficult to work with is not going to see you getting the opportunities you want. Further, it isn't going to see you building or nurturing relationships, which likely will lead to your isolation in the longer term. And these scenarios don't equal a career built on happy!

Emma's last piece of advice is to focus more on being a high performer, rather than a 'pro in place'. Emma defines a 'pro in place' as someone who is exceptional at their job. They know what they're doing and what needs to be done. They're technically astute and absolutely pros. Does it make them a high performer or high-potential employee? Not necessarily.

What takes someone from a pro in place to being a high performer then?

It's someone who brings people along with them. Someone who shares their knowledge with others and makes others good at their job because of it. Someone who really follows the principle of 'lifting others means you rise too'. Someone who lives the culture of the organisation and what it stands for. That's the difference.

Emma further adds that only being known for your technical skill will pigeonhole you, and you won't necessarily receive the broader growth opportunities that others do over the longer term.

So, what questions can you reflect on to work out where you sit? Here's what Emma recommends you ask yourself regularly:

- How am I contributing meaningfully outside of my individual tasks in ways that actually shift the needle forward?
- What am I doing to support and value others consistently?

- How am I investing in my relationships with others?

  How people view you and your performance at work is absolutely within your control. It's up to you as an individual to drive the direction of your career, and define and work that plan. Take the bull by the horns, make that meeting with your leader, and ask for a career conversation that you've taken the time to prepare for. Let them know what you want to do, where you want to go, the steps you're taking to get yourself there, and how you can support the business.

Couldn't have said it better myself.

Driving deeper work over shallow 'busyness': a conversation with Nikos Psaltopoulos

With decades of leadership experience across many teams and multiple continents, Nikos Psaltopoulos most recently finished his role as Chief Operating Officer at MarineTraffic (now Kpler), one of the world's leading maritime tech companies. MarineTraffic achieved huge growth, low turnover and certification as a Great Place to Work during Nikos's tenure there, so I wanted to understand from him what he thinks makes an employee an impact player, someone who can deliver without feeling like they're selling their soul.

I shared with Nikos my goal for this book – that is, for you to become clear on how you could not only show up inside your organisation in a way that is meaningful for you but also use traits that are valued by companies globally. I then pretended to be a genie and offered to grant Nikos three wishes for what all employees would do more of, and he summed up those wishes perfectly:

- empower themselves and take intentional action
- be cultural ambassadors
- have a sense of urgency.

On the idea of empowering themselves to take intentional action, Nikos believes:

In order to accelerate growth and move things forward, for individuals to grow, and therefore the company to grow, being stuck in a constant loop of seeking approval slows everything down. And that's why I look for the exact opposite and I want to instil the exact opposite in the individuals I work with.

Nikos acknowledged that leadership teams need to drive, nurture and encourage a culture of empowerment, but argued individuals also needed to 'step into the arena' and take responsibility for themselves and how they show up in the culture. He then continued on the idea of owning culture and why being a cultural ambassador is important to being seen, heard and valued at work:

Culture is everyone's responsibility. It's not solely my job to create the environment we all thrive in. We can create some principles and a framework of what great behaviours look like, but in order to bring that to life, we need everyone living by company values and understanding our vision. It's everyone's responsibility to be the culture that they want to thrive in. It's not the responsibility of one person; it's a shared responsibility. So, to me, those employees who really are culture ambassadors are just worth their weight in gold.

On his last wish to be granted, Nikos and I spoke about the idea of a sense of urgency. I was very keen to understand more about this element, given the often confused relationship between urgency and 'busyness', and the link to hustle culture:

A sense of urgency is not about running around proclaiming our busyness within the business and working on meaningless tasks and back-to-back meetings. Unfortunately, though, this has been a hangover from COVID, when the world went remote. To show our worth and our contribution, we all filled our diaries with meetings, because that gave us a level of presenteeism within the business. So, we were visible within the business and we were all stuck in meetings for most of the day. And it got us into a mode of doing lots of shallow work, and created a space where we were extending our working day because we spent the majority of our working hours on calls and then more time after that trying to catch up.

Just being present, though, doesn't actually mean that you are doing the work that's needed. It just means that you're there. So, the opportunity is to be really deliberate with how we invest our time and make it really clear in our heads that this is my 'shallow work' time and this is my 'deep work' time. And when I do shallow work, I'm working through my transactional tasks, my tick list, but then I have to make the intentional time for deep work that moves things forward.

Now that you've heard from other experts on what they believe makes a great employee, let's step into the first element of my five-part career framework designed to help you build your career on happy!

Chapter 3

Element one: Knowing yourself and setting your vision

'So, who are you beyond your job title?' Someone asked me this question once many years ago, and I struggled to answer it. I did what many people do when I ask the same question now – I restated my job title, tried to explain my job, and then listed off the other roles I played in life. Your other roles might include wife or husband, mother or father, daughter or son, and friend or sibling. These are not who you are, however; these are roles you play.

To create a career (and a life!) of happy rather than hustle, you've got to know yourself beyond just these roles. You've got to know the complex, multifaceted, layered person who sits beneath these roles. That's who you really are.

We all live and work in a society that prioritises asking 'What do you do for work?' before asking us how we are as a human. Think about it. How many networking events have you been to where you have the same conversation over and over again? It almost always starts with, 'What do you do?' Yes, this is lazy conversation, but it's also how we've been conditioned to engage over the years in the professional environment.

By that societal norm alone, is it any wonder that so many draw the conclusion that the status component of *what* we do and the title we hold is more important than *how* we deliver it – and more important than the person who sits behind the work?

In this first element of my five-part career framework, I ask you to dig deeper into who you are, what you value, and what your own personal definition of career success is. Why does this matter? Because in order to have a career built more on happy and less on hustle or hope, you've got to know and understand who you are, what your impact is and how your mindset plays into the actions you take. From there, you can set goals to bring your vision for success to life.

Let's go!

Know yourself to lead your career

Self-awareness is a key skill accessible to all of us that we can use to achieve almost anything we want in our lives – which is pretty damn cool, right? If you know yourself at your core, you are far more able to have a positive impact on yourself, your team and the people around you. You can use this knowledge to optimise your performance. However, again, we are often so focused on *what* we need to do, we forget about *how* we can do it in the most effective and energising way possible.

Think about the people you know inside your organisation for a moment. Now think about the ones you find the most difficult, inflexible or challenging to work with. Do you have someone in mind? What it is specifically about that person that you find difficult, challenging or inflexible? Almost always, their behaviour will be related to a lack of insight, or lack of understanding of why this insight matters.

This lack of insight may be due to either of the following:

- It's a blind spot and they really aren't aware of the impact they're having.
- They do know, but they just don't care.

Either way, this lack of insight and self-awareness will likely have a tangible impact on their ability to achieve and succeed in the long term if they continue to do nothing about it.

But seriously, what is self-awareness?

Daniel Goleman, a psychologist, author and world-renowned expert when it comes to teachings around self-awareness, defines it as 'having a deep understanding of one's emotions, strengths, weaknesses, needs, and drives'. Goleman goes onto argue:

> *People with strong self-awareness are neither overly critical nor unrealistically hopeful. Rather, they are honest – with themselves and with others. People who have a high degree of self-awareness recognize how their feelings affect them, other people, and their job performance.*

For example, a self-aware person would know that lacking clarity on a project brings about significant stress for them, so they would ensure they allow 'buffer' time with their key stakeholders for clarifying questions to help ease their stress and enable them to deliver a better result.

A self-aware person may also know that what is really important to them in their career is autonomy and flexibility. This awareness means they won't get swept up in a great recruiter 'job sell' for a new role that might offer more money but does not provide any real flexibility – beyond them being able to arrive between 8.15 am and 8.30 am every day. The self-aware person can consider whether the position aligns with their career values and then make the right decision for them.

A self-aware leader knows that when they are feeling overwhelmed they have a tendency to focus on micro-details to feel more in control, but that this makes their colleagues feel micromanaged. So, instead, the leader communicates more consistently with the team about the challenges they're facing and relevant deadlines. This helps the leader feel more at ease, and their team continues to feel trusted, empowered and involved.

Lastly, a self-aware person knows the impact that their current attitude and mindset is having on their motivation and wellbeing, and on the people around them. So, they intentionally create space for themselves to re-energise as needed, instead of just 'pushing through'.

Over to you. What do you know about yourself?

Your Happy Career Action

Here are some self-reflection questions for you to consider. You can answer them in the context of your career and your life, and I encourage you to write your thoughts down in a journal or notebook. You can then continue building on them as you progress through this book.

See what comes up when you ask yourself the following:

- What are your strengths and weaknesses?
- What motivates you? What excites you? What drains you?
- What makes you feel stressed or frustrated at work, and how do you behave when you are feeling triggered?
- What five words would you use to describe yourself? What do these look like as behaviours and actions with others?

- What are some of your core beliefs, or things you believe to be true? Where do they come from? What is it about them that you see as truth? What else have you considered?

'Can I tick self-awareness off the list now?'

When I run workshops around self-awareness, I'm often asked something along the lines of, 'When is the whole self-awareness thing done? When can I tick that off my focus list?' What do you think my answer is? Never. Learning about yourself is never done.

You will continue to be put in situations you haven't navigated before – in work and in life. And these situations will bring you into territories where different parts of yourself will come forward. In order to navigate those situations as effectively as possible and get the best outcomes for yourself, your team and your organisation, you have to be self-aware. You must remain open and curious about yourself.

If that isn't enough of a reason to always be learning about yourself, maybe this is: the World Economic Forum *Future of Jobs Report 2023* listed self-awareness as one of the top four core skills required of workers in our current and future workforces. That means putting an intentional focus on self-awareness is not only good from the perspective of creating humans who are more aware of who they are, how they engage and what lights them up, it is also a core skill valued by your workplace.

I hate to burst your bubble, but self-awareness is a team sport, yo!

In her 2017 TEDx Talk 'Increase your self-awareness with one simple fix', organisational psychologist Dr Tasha Eurich claims, 'There are two types of people: those who think they are self-aware, and those who really are'. Dr Eurich goes on to say that she and her team have established through their research that although

95 per cent of people think they are self-aware, only 10 to 15 per cent of us actually are.

Hold the flippin' phone. Seriously? Only 10 to 15 per cent? Because here's the thing: self-awareness is more than just introspection. In fact, too much introspection and rumination can work against you, particularly if you have a tendency to be a HAPP (high-achieving people-pleaser) – an acronym coined and backed with research by confidence and self-respect expert Dr Katherine Iscoe.

You see, self-awareness is more than just looking in the mirror and deciding what you think you see. Self-awareness is a team sport. In order to be truly self-aware, you need to know how others see you too. How is your intention translating to impact? Is how you see yourself also how others see you?

Dr Eurich goes on to explain that two types of self-awareness also exist: internal and external.

Internal self-awareness guides you on your own values, passions, aspirations and beliefs. Importantly, Dr Eurich and her research team have found that strong levels of internal self-awareness are associated with higher job and relationship satisfaction, personal and social control, and happiness.

Of equal importance is the second category of self-awareness: external. This means you also know how other people view you against the same factors, such as values and beliefs. Dr Eurich's research demonstrates that people who know how others see them are more skilled at showing empathy and taking others' perspectives. When leaders see themselves as their employees or colleagues do, their employees and peers tend to have a better relationship with them, feel more satisfied with them, and see them as more effective in general.

So, how do you generate high levels of self-awareness in both categories?

Asking what, not why

To gain more productive, constructive and, ultimately, useful insights from both yourself and those around you, Dr Eurich suggests asking *what* questions rather than *why* questions. Asking a 'why' question is comparable to looking in a rear-view mirror – it keeps you stuck in the past, wondering how things could have been different. Asking a 'what' question is more like looking through the windshield ahead – it acknowledges where you are right now and keeps you moving forward constructively.

Table 1 provides some examples of how you can change 'why?' questions to 'what? questions to lead yourself to some self-awareness insights.

Table 1: Turning 'why?' questions into 'what?' questions

From	To
Why do I feel this way?	What specific thoughts or events triggered my emotions? What do I think could be done differently to manage or cope with these emotions more effectively?
Why did I lose my sh*t like that?	What do I need to be more aware of in the future to avoid this happening again?
Why did you say this about me?	What steps can I take in the future to do a better job of supporting or collaborating with you?

The best leaders have taken the baggage off their backs

The best leaders I have ever worked with and for not only knew the power of self-awareness but were also actively engaged in the regular pursuit of new insights. These leaders were more engaging and more enthusiastic about their work, and better empowered their teams, because they knew enough about themselves to know how to target their efforts, enthusiasm and expertise to get the best results from themselves and their teams.

It was as though they'd taken off their metaphorical backpack and no longer had the weight of it on their shoulders. Too many leaders are burdened and burnt out by the baggage they are carrying around, thinking they need to have it all together. These leaders, on the other hand, were open and honest about their shortcomings, and then actively surrounded themselves with people who could plug their gaps – and they were happier for it. They were able to focus more on the things they were passionate about and leverage their strengths and talents. They thrived because of this self-awareness, and so did their teams.

As Ernest Hemingway stated, 'You can't get away from yourself by moving from one place to another'. The best leaders acknowledge that they can't drive greater performance in their teams, colleagues or organisations until they are able to truly sit, reflect and understand themselves and their own minds.

The power of mindset and breaking through barriers

Claire, nobody will give you what you're worth. They will give you what they think you are worth. You are the one who controls their thinking.

Remember those personal career lessons (and career-limiting moves) I shared in chapter 2? Well, this is another lesson I benefited from. A mentor shared this statement with me at the exact time I was feeling unsure about my place, position and impact inside the organisation I was working for.

I felt down, out of my depth and completely disheartened by the constant level of change and disruption I was experiencing. And it absolutely dented my confidence. This then became the prism I was looking at the world through – negative, unhelpful, exhausting and isolating. This was the reality I had created for myself, and just about every aspect of my life was suffering because of it.

The feedback from my mentor wasn't specific to aspects such as pay or promotions. It wasn't only relevant to a corporate role, either. It was, and still is, relevant to every area of life. People will only give you what they think you are worth. You are the one who controls their thinking. What this also means, though, is that you must know and believe in your own worth. You need to know and believe in what *you* bring to the table.

When you are in the grips of constant change, disruption and instability, though, knowing your worth can feel really hard. You're more likely to feel as if you are on a constant tightrope walk, just waiting to fall off. Every time you think you've broken through the discomfort, some new challenge seems to appear.

Turning a spotlight on the devil in your mind

When you feel unsure, unsafe or under threat, your brain tries to keep you safe and free from harm by activating the 'fight, flight or freeze' response. As much as technology has evolved over the last few centuries, our brains have not evolved to the same level. In the modern world, we are no longer being chased by tigers as our ancestors once were, but our brains still assess fear and respond in the same way, and they do what they think they need to do to keep us safe.

Often, your brain tries to keep you safe by telling you stories, consciously and unconsciously. It uses these stories to put just enough doubt in your mind – about your ability to do something, not do something, say something, not say something or take a 'risk' – to stop you doing anything that makes you uncomfortable or 'unsafe'.

Enter some of the truly nasty things that we can say to ourselves that ultimately stop us taking effective action.

You know the voice I'm talking about.

I'm talking about the little gremlin that sneaks up on you just as you are about to embark on something new – perhaps a fresh challenge, or a new idea or opinion you are ready to share with your colleagues. Right as you are going to put yourself out there, the little voice pops up.

It might say things like, 'Are you sure you want to do this? You'll look ridiculous if you get it wrong'. Maybe it cuts deeper and says something like, 'Who are you to honestly think you can sit at this table with these people? They have so much more experience than you'. This voice reins you back in, keeping you stuck and holding you back from playing bigger. Maybe it stops you from even playing at all.

This inner critic can pop up anywhere. Its goal is often to try to hinder any and all progression you're striving to make, particularly if it involves trying something new. You might even be so used to living with this voice that you don't realise the impact it's having on you – and all it's taking away. We rarely question the validity and truth of what those voices are trying to say to us. We just believe, and then act accordingly – which, ironically, often means not to act at all.

Silencing your inner critic

I was going to say that... but then I didn't.

Have you ever wanted to share something in a meeting – perhaps an idea, an opinion or a recommendation about something – but you didn't say it out loud? You held back because that little inner critic made you believe you'd sound stupid if you were wrong, that you had no value to add to the conversation, or whatever other baloney they came up with. And while you're sitting there having an internal dialogue about everything that could go wrong if you said your thoughts out loud, have you ever had someone else swoop in and do just that? They shared the same idea or opinion that you were so busy talking yourself out of sharing that you never said it out loud!

What then happens? The crowd goes wild, of course! Meanwhile, you're now sitting there berating yourself even more for not saying anything sooner. Sound familiar? Yep, me too.

Stories, self-talk or narratives we often tell ourselves when we feel scared, uncomfortable or anxious can include the following:

- 'I'm not good/smart/talented enough to do this.'
- 'I'll never be as successful as Janet; I don't have that kind of luck.'
- 'I'm not smart enough to achieve my career goals.'
- 'I tried it once and it didn't work, so why bother again?'
- 'I'm too old/young to do this – no-one will take me seriously.'
- 'I'll just fail anyway, so why bother?'
- 'I'm too shy to put myself out there.'
- 'What if people don't like me?'
- 'I just don't have the right connections to succeed.'
- 'I'm not lucky; good things never happen to me.'
- 'I'll never be able to learn all of this.'
- 'I don't have the resources to pursue my dreams.'

- 'I'm too busy; I don't have time to try something different.'
- 'Others will judge and criticise me.'
- 'I can't change; this is just the way I am.'
- 'Success is only for others, not for me.'
- 'I'll never advance because I don't have the same technical skills as they do.'
- 'I'm not good at public speaking, so I'll never be able to present my ideas effectively.'
- 'I'm not good at self-promotion, so my achievements will always go unnoticed.'
- 'I'll never find a fulfilling career because I prioritise financial stability over passion.'
- 'No-one will ever really recognise me here because I'm just a small part of a big organisation.'
- 'I'll never be successful because I don't have any mentors or sponsors.'
- 'I'll never be promoted because I don't have a degree from a prestigious university.'
- 'I'll never stand out because I'm too introverted to network effectively.'

Do any of these resonate with you? What's sad about these kinds of statements is that we'd never say them to a friend – and if a friend said something like this about themselves, we'd likely whip them into shape pretty quickly, and remind them about how fabulous they are and everything they've achieved in their lives.

Your thoughts and beliefs impact your feelings, which impact your actions and, therefore, your results. Imagine if you're saying those kinds of thoughts to and about yourself regularly. What impact do you think that is going to have on your confidence? How will it affect your ability to back yourself and to act? And what impact might it have on your courage to take risks in your career or your life?

This is not new information. Any number of books about cognitive behavioural therapy (CBT) outline the impact of different thinking patterns, but I want you to specifically consider the impact your thoughts (and, therefore, actions) may be having on how you see your career and leadership opportunities.

If your thoughts aren't liberating, they become the prism – or prison – that you let yourself live in. This prism becomes your reality, and you will likely continue to resist change, not take risks, and not believe that you can learn or grow.

This is a fixed mindset. To succeed, though (in whatever way you define success), you need to develop a growth mindset.

Grow your mind, grow your career

In *Mindset: Changing the way you think to fulfil your potential*, psychologist Carol Dweck talks about the differences between having a fixed and a growth mindset.

A growth mindset is something we can all benefit from. Why? Because it means that we are able to see growth in setbacks and the learning opportunity in any failure, and ultimately, that we believe we can get better at things through grit and perseverance.

A fixed mindset, on the other hand, can restrain us and hold us back from bigger and better things in our careers and in our lives. A fixed mindset means we don't believe we can learn and grow – we hold an 'if we weren't born with it, we will never have it' approach to things. It also means we are less open to feedback and to seeing challenges as opportunities that we can surpass.

Are you permanently in one mindset or the other? Absolutely not – you're human, after all. So, you will drift into a fixed mindset at times – usually when you are uncomfortable! However, being more aware when this happens is a key enabler of a career built more on happy and less on hustle. This awareness can help you see the opportunities you want and actually believe that you can take advantage of them.

Your beliefs impact every decision you make

Now that you've started digging deeper into who you are and what lights you up, it's also a great time to start reflecting on some of the career beliefs you hold. Understanding what these beliefs are, where they come from and, ultimately, whether they are constraining or liberating you is a great place to start.

For example, say you believe the following: 'No way could I apply for that role because I haven't 100 per cent done everything on the job ad before.' Holding the belief that you must satisfy 100 per cent of the criteria on a job advertisement before you give yourself permission to put your hat in the ring, or even have a further conversation about it, means you may be missing out on opportunities, or pitching yourself for opportunities below your capability.

What about this belief: 'I can't ask to be a part of that project – what if they say no?' Hesitating to ask to be involved in a project out of fear of rejection reflects a mindset rooted in 'what if?' scenarios and apprehension. While you have no guarantee of a positive outcome, by expressing interest and making an effort, you increase the likelihood of success. Taking action, even if it leads to a 'no', can still open doors to other opportunities and make your intentions known to others, potentially leading to favourable outcomes in the future.

To challenge your beliefs and take more constructive action, ask yourself the following:

· Is this belief true? If it is, how do I know?
· Is it constraining me or liberating me?
· What else could be true?

- If I did take action on this belief, what is the worst that could happen? If that did happen, what could I do?
- What is the best outcome that could happen, and what would that mean for me and my career?

Own your story, manage your mind.

When you have a deeper understanding of who you are, what you've done and what you are capable of, managing your inner critic and overpowering the constraining or unhelpful thoughts attempting to keep you stuck becomes easier. You are more able to reframe these thoughts with constructive, rational and fact-based thoughts, empowering you to move forward with action. You can provide evidence of ways you have completed hard things before, and what you learnt from those experiences, to continue to propel yourself forward. You can remind yourself that you have already survived your hardest days, and that perhaps taking this next brave step, such as applying for a role you really want, won't be so bad either. Through knowing yourself and your story, you can know your mind – and then better manage it to support you in ways that are helpful.

Over to you.

Your Happy Career Action

Take out your journal and reflect on the following questions:

- What achievements are you proudest of in your life?
- What strengths and wisdom did you rely on to accomplish those achievements?
- Who has played a critical role in your life and helped shape you to be the person you are?
- What significant events have shaped you and how?

- What challenges have you faced along the way and how did you navigate them?
- What did you learn from these challenges?
- When have you felt at your best?
- When have you felt at your worst, and how did you get past it?
- What wisdom can you remind yourself of next time you are facing a new challenge?

Establishing your career values

Your alarm goes off and you automatically hit snooze. It goes off again. Snooze. You eventually get up with this feeling of heaviness. You drag your feet to the bathroom to start getting ready for the day. You think, *Hmmmmm, it's Wednesday, hump day – YES! Only two more days after today to get through until the weekend*. Have you ever felt as if you're only living for your weekends? Often, this happens when you aren't working in a career that's aligned with your values. There's a gap, or a misalignment – and that almost certainly leads to a career built on hustle and not on happy.

Your career values are the principles and beliefs that are most important to you in your professional life. Not having a clear vision of what your career values are is like building a house without a building plan. You grab items that look like they might work, but you don't have any real strategy for how things all need to come together or how to build a strong foundation. You simply *hope* things work out.

Without a map, you fly blind

Without the guidance of your values, you leave yourself open to the influence of others based on who has the best sell, instead of being true to yourself and listening to what is important to you.

Your career values might include autonomy, creativity, financial stability, work-life balance, social impact and personal growth. When you have clarity on these values, they act as your driving force and a map for your career. With your career values front of mind, you're more able to identify opportunities that align with your goals and priorities, and make choices that support your definition of career success and happiness.

Do you highly value creativity and innovation? If so, you might seek out a career opportunity that allows you to express your ideas and contribute to the development of new products or services. If you instead value work-life integration, you might prioritise workplaces that offer *truly* flexible schedules or *actual* remote work options. Also keep in mind that your career values change over time, so take the time to check in with yourself regularly and identify your key career values.

Let me tell you about Caitlin as an example here. Caitlin came to me feeling unmotivated, stuck and a bit disenchanted by her current role in marketing. She had been in this position and organisation for fewer than six months, after leaving her previous role because of the same feelings of being stuck, unfulfilled and as if she was lacking meaning. Caitlin's new role had offered a bigger salary and greater flexibility. Thinking, *Surely a change of scenery and a new organisation is what I need*, she'd jumped at it. But now those same feelings were back.

Caitlin had done what many of us do when that sinking feeling creeps in – she had run *away* from something, instead of running *towards* something with clarity and enthusiasm.

My first question to Caitlin when she contacted me was, 'What are your career values?' Her reply was, 'What do you mean?' Often when we find ourselves in a space of dissatisfaction or apathy in our roles, we think that scrolling job boards and picking the best of what we can see is the right next step. Enter an engaging, well-written job ad with some bolded perks and the promise of a 'competitive salary' and we jump in without question – only to find ourselves in the same position again months later. This is why career values are so important. They allow you to make calculated decisions based on your principles first, and not force yourself into a box that was never meant for you to fit into.

Over to you. What are your career values?

Your Happy Career Action

I've provided a list of 84 possible career values. To start gaining clarity on what your career values are, scan this list and circle the ten words that resonate the most with you when you think about the kind of career you want to create for yourself. Think about how you want to feel about the work you do, the kind of environment you want to be in, and the way you want to show up in it. Also think about these career values more broadly in the context of the life you want to create for yourself. This is not an exhaustive list by any means, so if a word is not included that feels meaningful to you, be sure to capture it for yourself.

Potential career values

Acceptance	Boldness	Contribution
Accountability	Bravery	Creativity
Achievement	Candour	Curiosity
Adaptability	Challenge	Dependability
Adventure	Clarity	Determination
Authenticity	Collaboration	Diversity
Authority	Compassion	Empathy
Autonomy	Communication	Enthusiasm
Balance	Community	Equality

Family	Loyalty	Security
Fairness	Meaningful work	Self-improvement
Financial stability	Optimism	Simplicity
Flexibility	Ownership	Social impact
Friendship	Participation	Spirituality
Growth	Patience	Stability
Happiness	Peace	Status
Hard work	Persistence	Success
Honesty	Personal growth	Sustainability
Humility	Popularity	Teamwork
Humour	Power	Tenacity
Impact	Quality	Time management
Improvement	Recognition	Transparency
Ingenuity	Relationships	Trustworthiness
Innovation	Reliability	Wealth
Kindness	Reputation	Wisdom
Knowledge	Respect	Work ethic
Leadership	Responsibility	Work-life balance
Learning	Results	Zest

You may look at this list and think, *But all of these things are important!* Yes, they are – but not all of them are going to be of equal importance to you. How you define each word may also be different from someone else, and that's okay too.

Once you've circled your ten values, order them from one to ten, with one being the most important value to you, the absolute non-negotiable that you need to have a career built on happy and not on hustle.

Next, grab your top five values and write down what they each mean to you. What does that value specifically look like when you're living it?

One last note – if you notice yourself gravitating to any words because you think you should, try to catch yourself and reflect on whether this is truly a career value that is important to you or one that society tends to push as a metric of success.

Capturing your career values

Your career values don't need to make sense to anyone but you. If you are clear on what they are, and what it looks and feels like for you to be living these values, you're more able to make better decisions for yourself and your career going forward.

Need an example to help finalise your top five? Here are my five career values and what they mean to me:

- **Growth.** I value learning and growth enormously, and I believe that when we stop learning we become stale. Therefore, I need to be in environments and working on opportunities that enable me to grow and learn. Does that also mean I fail? Yep, but I see that as being a metric of growth. If I am living the same day repeatedly, I get bored and I lose motivation, so I look for ways in my business (and life!) to continue to stretch myself.

- **Contribution (impact).** I believe that we are on this earth to do more than make money and pay bills, and so when I consider the work I am involved with, I ask myself, 'Is this leaving the world in a better place than I found it?' and, 'How am I making a meaningful contribution here?' For me to feel motivated and valued, I've realised over the years I need to feel like I am making a meaningful contribution.

- **Humour and heart.** An enormous value of mine is working with people and in environments where we can do serious work but don't need to take ourselves too seriously. Life is too short not to love and laugh deeply. I thrive in situations where I can be laughing one minute and in a deep exchange about the meaning of life the next. For me, this has also meant surrounding myself with people in my own business who also value these exchanges.

- **Authenticity (relatability).** I like real talk – human to human. I believe that the quicker we all cut the crap and lessen the corporate jargon, the quicker we can have people operating as their best selves. Over the years, this value has meant I have had to make some decisions about the kinds of organisations I can work with and those I can't.

- **Enthusiasm.** I thrive on enthusiasm. I die in environments that just feel grey and sterile. I believe that if you're one foot in and one foot out, you are nowhere, which means I like to do things all the way or none of the way – with enthusiasm and zest. So I make sure I work with clients who are enthusiastic about the work that we do, and that I am engaging in projects that I can be fully enthusiastic about, and not just 'ticking a box'.

Defining success on your terms

What makes someone successful? What makes someone unsuccessful? What makes life a success? Who gets to decide? And how do we define success in our own life?

Many of us never take the time to think about what our unique definition of success is for our own lives and, more importantly, who we want to be and how we want to show up in our own lives. Instead, we allow media and marketing tactics to dictate to us what success *should* look like – how we *should* measure our lives, and what we *should* measure our lives against.

However, adopting this approach is a seriously flawed strategy, because it is based purely on listening to external sources, all with their own agendas (to sell to you!), telling you what you should value, instead of you listening to yourself first and foremost. This strategy operates from the outside in, not the inside out.

Going from the inside out and getting clear on your personal definition of success is a key part of establishing a career built more on happy and less on hustle. In conjunction with your values, your definition of success provides the foundation for knowing what you want from your own career and your own life. Once you can see the vision, you can put the targeted actions in place to go and get it; this, in turn, increases enthusiasm.

Working out what you truly need

Maybe you've heard the parable of the fisherman and the business-man. Here is the express version of it:

Once upon a time, in a small coastal village, there lived a humble fisherman. Every day, he would wake up early, row his small boat out to sea, and catch just enough fish to feed his family. With each passing day, he found contentment in his simple yet fulfilling life.

One day, while the fisherman was mending his nets by the shore, a wealthy businessman from the city approached him.

'Good sir,' said the businessman, 'Why do you spend your days toiling away for so little reward? With your skill, you could catch more fish, sell them at the market and make a fortune. Then, you could buy a bigger boat, hire others to fish for you, and expand your enterprise. Eventually, you could even build your own fishing empire'.

The fisherman listened politely and then asked, 'But what would I do after that?'

The businessman replied, 'Why, you could retire to this peaceful village, wake up late, fish a little, play with your children, take siestas with your wife, and enjoy life's simple pleasures'.

The fisherman smiled. 'But that's exactly what I'm doing now.'

With that, the fisherman returned to his boat, content in the knowledge that he already possessed everything he truly needed: a loving family, meaningful work, and the beauty of the sea.

Let's forgive ourselves first.

In a society that thrives off hustle, you can be forgiven for forgetting that life is much more than what you own and what you have. The dollars in your bank account aren't a measure of your own worth as a human being or how meaningful your contribution is to the world – but we all can forget that sometimes. This is why clarifying your values and then devising your personal definition of success helps you stay on track to creating a career and a life that is meaningful to you.

Maybe your definition of success is to create amazing art that lights up the homes of people across the world, without needing a big home or lots of things to fit into it for yourself.

Maybe your definition of success is to be a midwife and help bring new life into the world. You know you'll work crazy shifts and crazy hours, so your version of success also means having a home away from the hustle and bustle and noise. You want a sanctuary of peace where you can just be.

Maybe your definition of success is a warm, loving home, full of children, that smells like amazing baked treats every day, and has a warm fire and a backyard to play in. You want work that guarantees flexibility so you can prioritise your children above all else.

Maybe you know that impact is one of your values, and so your definition of success is being able to help drive positive change for vulnerable people who need support, while also maintaining kindness and compassion. The specific job that provides this is less important to you.

My point here is that success looks different for everyone, and so it should. We're all created differently. What matters is that you get clear on what success means to you.

Personal priorities play a part too

Part of curating your definition of success involves understanding what your personal priorities are. Your career doesn't happen inside a vacuum, and to thrive in a career built more on happy and less on hustle, you need to be clear on how your career supports your other life priorities.

For example, my personal priorities include:

- a working life where I can choose (for the most part) how, when and where to work, without having to be fixed to a Monday to Friday, 9 am to 5 pm timetable
- the ability to take at least one big holiday per year and extra-long weekend getaways every couple of months
- Mondays and Fridays that aren't client-facing and allow me to start my days with a focus on wellness
- the ability to support my family as my parents get older.

Over to you. What does success mean to you?

Your Happy Career Action

Reflect on and answer the following questions to help you get closer to defining your own personal definition of success:

- What is your definition of success for your own career and life? (Your career values should help you here.)

- When you close your eyes and imagine that definition, what do you see? How do you feel?
- What are your personal priorities that need to be considered?
- Thirty years from now, when you look back, how do you want to have lived and who do you want to be remembered as?

That's the first element of my five-part career framework. So, what have you learnt? What changes do you need to consider? What steps can you take now to help you move closer to a career built more on happy and less on hustle and hope?

Key takeaways

TL;DR (too long, didn't read)? It's okay, here's the first element in a nutshell:

- Self-awareness is the first step to building a career on happy. You've got to know yourself to lead yourself.
- Understanding your own mindset and beliefs, and the stories your inner critic can tell you, helps you take targeted action to move yourself forward in your career in ways you can be proud of.
- Your career values are the essence of what you need to be 'in play' for you to thrive, and will help you make more empowered career decisions.
- Getting clear on your personal definition of career success can help you stay on track, even when the road gets a little bumpy and uncertain.

Chapter 4

Element two:
Cultivating your bold brand

The less hustle, more happy career owner thrives off a positive, credible brand, because they know that a strong brand equals a strong career with opportunities to grow and develop.

In this second element of my five-part career framework, I look at how you can cultivate a bold brand that feels authentic to you – a brand that sees you leveraging your strengths, talents and experiences to get outcomes. I look at how you can build your own unique selling proposition (USP) and stand out for the reasons that you choose.

But first, let's have a look at how you can stand out for the wrong reasons.

Your brand is more than what people say about you

You may have heard the phrase, popularised by Jeff Bezos, that 'your brand is what people say about you when you're not in the room'. Well, I believe that in a work context, your brand is more than just what people say about you – it's about what they don't say, too. And it's also about what they do, or don't do, around you *because* of your brand.

Let me introduce you to Georgia…

'Don't bother asking Georgia – you'll never get anything back on time!' A colleague said this to me when I was hoping to get some assistance with updating my access. I was fairly new to the organisation at the time and didn't know the lay of the land just yet.

'What do you mean?' I said.

'Georgia is renowned for not responding to emails or coming back to people. You want it done, you will literally have to stand at her desk and watch it be done', I was told.

Right, I thought to myself as I headed downstairs to see Georgia. As I approached, I could almost see the 'dammit, don't make eye contact' look on her face as she hoped that maybe I didn't actually see her at her desk and would just walk past her.

'Hey, Georgia. How are you?' I said with a big smile.

'Fine', was the best she could come up with, not looking up from her computer.

'I'm having some issues getting access to this system, and I'm told you are the person here who makes things happen. I'd be so grateful for your help'.

Georgia looked up at me as if I had just given her the first compliment she had ever received in her life. Her demeanour completely changed. She sat up a little straighter, and the 'bracing for impact' look she'd had when I first arrived all but vanished.

Once she'd helped me with my task, I decided, somewhat puzzled by the quick change I had just witnessed, that I would dig a little deeper with Georgia in the hope that maybe it would help. I knew it was a risk, but I felt I could either contribute to the toxic conversion about Georgia or try to give her some feedback with kindness and clarity as the intention.

'Georgia, I've just found you super helpful, but that's not the side of you others seem to see as much around here. Is that something you're aware of?'

Georgia looked at me and sighed.

'Yes, I know that,' she said. 'People here don't see the side of me that I want them to see, but I'm just so busy and it feels too late now. Even if I tried to change, people wouldn't believe me – so why bother?'

What Georgia misunderstood was that people believe what they can see. How people perceive you and your brand may not always be who you are. Instead, your brand is formed by what people see and then believe, based on the consistency (or lack thereof) in the way you show up. Is this fair? No, not always. However, it does give you even more reason to deliberately show the parts of yourself that you do want people to see – the parts you're proud of and that make you *you*.

Think about someone you work with who, when you delegate something to them or collaborate on something with them, you know the task is absolutely going to be completed, and to a high standard. You know your colleague has it sorted, and you can basically cross the task off your own to-do list, both literally and mentally, safe in the knowledge it is covered. That reliability is part of your colleague's brand – along with credibility and, therefore, trust. You trust them.

Now think about that colleague you work with who is perhaps similar to Georgia in my example, where they don't give you that same feeling of confidence. After delegating a task to them, you can't cross it off your mental or literal list, because you'll likely need to follow up, check in and ensure the work is being completed, either on time or to the level that's needed. This is a brand too – albeit not a great one.

And, finally, think about this:

Opportunities do or don't come your way because of how you are perceived inside your organisation.

You may think your brand is based on superficial things such as your title, email footer, what you wear or the thumbnail picture people see in internal communications. However, your brand is so much more than these things.

Your brand is your reputation

In 2016, I was fortunate enough to attend the Zappos Culture Camp, hosted onsite at Zappos HQ in Las Vegas by the late Tony Hsieh. Hsieh was the CEO of Zappos, a US-based online marketplace, for 21 years. Prior to joining Zappos, Hsieh co-founded the internet advertising network LinkExchange, which he sold to Microsoft in 1998 for $265 million. Although many have argued that Hsieh had some eclectic ways of working and doing business, few disputed his ability to grow and nurture an incredible company culture. I attended the Zappos Culture Camp to learn more about how the Zappos culture and the company had been able to consistently attract people from all over the world to work with and learn from them.

Zappos's core purpose is 'to live and deliver WOW'. It's no surprise, then, that its number-one core company value is 'Deliver WOW through service'. When I read that for the first time, I recall thinking, *That's nice*, but I also felt I'd heard similar company statements a thousand times before, so I didn't necessarily believe it to be true.

When I arrived on day one of the culture camp, though, I saw this proclamation come to life. In front of me on my table was a wheel of Australian brie cheese, Ritz crackers, and a Hershey's Cookies 'n' Creme bar. These were all things I'd said I loved in a passing comment to the organiser of the camp before arriving. (You also talk to random strangers about food you like to eat on all your phone calls, right?) And when I looked around the room, every person had a unique snack, treat, toy or other merchandise in front of them.

Talk about delivering WOW through service and proving your reputation!

Clarity and consistency create capital

Think about some of the best brand experiences you've had. What was it about them that made them memorable? I bet it wasn't the fact that the last pair of Nikes you bought were comfortable – you expect that as a given. I'm also sure your last memorable experience wasn't the restaurant that served your meal nice and hot – again, duh. No, when it comes to memorable experiences that make us feel valued, they are almost always due to the small but unexpected things that show us a brand's true commitment.

The same is true for you. Your brand isn't built by something you do one time. It's built in the moments of consistency, and in the moments that are meaningful.

It's one thing to say you are customer-focused, for example; it's another to show that through your actions.

Choose what you want to represent

I once worked with an executive of one of Australia's largest organisations. One day I asked her, 'What would you like your brand to represent?' Her response was brilliant.

She said 'calm'.

She went on to talk about how she wanted her brand to represent the calm in the chaos – the stability in the ambiguity, the firm hand on shaky ground.

The next part of our conversation was around how she could bring this brand to life consistently and leverage it through her strengths and actions. Having a strong personal and professional brand starts with getting really clear on who you are, what you stand for, and what impact you want to have on others. (Hello, element one!) Next, it is about reflecting on how the actions you take demonstrate this consistently.

The more real you are about who you are and how you show up, the more authentic your brand will be to those around you, the better results you'll see, and the better you'll feel about how you're showing up.

A**holes and authenticity are not the same thing

Let's be clear, though, that cultivating and nurturing a strong and authentic brand is *not* a licence to be an a**hole. Behaving poorly or disrespectfully in the workplace under the banner of being 'authentic' is a sure-fire way to do the opposite of what you think you're doing.

Being truly authentic means truly knowing yourself, including your weaknesses, and continuing to be accountable in those moments when you can do better. For example, a personal value of yours might be honesty; however, being brutal or unkind to a colleague under the guise of 'honesty' and 'authenticity' does not make you a strong leader. Authenticity still requires you to exercise strong judgement, social awareness and an ability to build trust with others through sharing yourself.

Role models are clues in the game of brand building

'Who are your role models, Claire'? A coach once asked me this question and I couldn't answer it. In fact, if I am really honest, at that time in my career I don't think I saw value in the concept of role models. It all felt a bit 'fluffy'.

Now, though, I see the real value of role models – and it's so much more than just being able to name them when asked. Having clarity on role models is not just about having someone you admire who you can learn from and be guided by. Your role models are a mirror for the heart of your own leadership values.

The behaviours you admire in others are often the things that you value too, and sometimes even character strengths that you hold within yourself. Reflecting on role models intentionally shines a light on this, and enables you to deliberately translate those behaviours you admire in others into a leadership style that is reflective (and authentic) of you. Role models help you define with more clarity what you want your brand to represent.

Over to you. Who are your role models?

Your Happy Career Action

Reflect on and write down three to five role models you've had across your life. You don't have to have known them personally. They can be anyone – family members, sports stars, celebrities, politicians or leaders you've worked with previously or currently.

Once you've written down your role models, also write what it is about each one that makes them a role model to you. What values do they represent? How do you see them demonstrate these? And why is that important to you?

Building your own unique selling proposition (USP)

Whether you are a self-proclaimed 'Swiftie' or not, you would have to have been living under some sort of rock not to know who Taylor

Swift is and the massive impact her brand has had globally. But it will likely surprise you to learn you're not that different from Tay Tay.

Want to know what you and Taylor Swift have in common?

Over her 20-year career, Taylor Swift's profile has grown considerably, and her experience as a singer has too. At last check she had worked within country, pop, folk and rock genres, but even with these career evolutions, or eras, the consistency of her personal brand has remained the same.

Taylor Swift has kept the same beliefs and values that have made her *her* since the beginning. She remains relatable and open, often sharing insights into her personal life and challenges through her songs and at her concerts. She is idealistic, heartfelt and optimistic, empowering fans to feel that they can be that way too. And although her concerts now attract hundreds of thousands more fans around the globe than when she started, she still has 'Swifties' leaving her concerts feeling like they saw the real Taylor Swift.

Although Taylor Swift's experience has grown, the way she shows up has remained largely the same. She's remained vigilant and intentional about her own unique selling proposition (USP) – and you can too.

Highlighting your uniqueness

Experts often talk about the concept of a USP in relation to products and services, yet we rarely think about it with regard to ourselves. You likely know that to consistently sell, brands must highlight their USP and establish enough credibility to convince you that you want to engage with them. However, have you invested this kind of time and attention on the most important product of all – yourself?

Getting clear on your professional and personal brand is a journey that requires patience, perseverance and time to reflect, dig deep and get real with yourself. Equally, though, it is one of the most liberating and confidence-enhancing journeys you will ever invest in. It allows you to know, own and leverage your unique strengths more than almost anything else. And uncovering your USP will help you build deeper confidence and clarity on who you are and what value you bring to the organisations you work in.

Best of all, out of the 8 billion people on the planet, you are the only one who carries your exact USP. Not one other person on the planet has the exact same experiences, worldviews, beliefs and presence that you bring. Pretty cool, right?

I've developed the following formula to build out a professional USP that sticks:

Experiences + thought leadership + presence
= unique selling proposition

Here's a bit more detail on each of the three elements that make up your USP:

- **Experiences.** What are the pivotal career and life experiences that have shaped you and led you to where and who you are today? These could include particular opportunities you've had, a travel experience, adversity you've navigated and your upbringing. I know that some of the most challenging times in my life have also been the key moments and experiences that have shaped me. I wouldn't be where I am today without them.

- **Thought leadership.** What are your personal beliefs, values and thoughts that impact how you show up? How do you see the world? These beliefs and values also make you uniquely you. They ultimately inform how you see things and how you share your story. They will be different from the person next to you, and that is okay.

- **Presence.** Consider what kind of 'vibe' you want to radiate or impact you want to have on people. How do you want to make others feel? What tone do you want to set when you walk into a room? This is not a trick question. Yes, likely 99 per cent of people want to have a positive impact on others. However, I want you to get more specific than that. Think back to the example I included earlier in this chapter of the executive who wanted to be calm in the chaos. That is a form of presence.

To give you an example of how these elements work together, table 2 outlines my responses in each of the three areas.

Table 2: Combining experiences, thought leadership and presence

Experiences	Thought leadership	Presence
Being promoted into a senior general manager role at a very young age in a company going through mergers and acquisitions. Having skin cancer in 2019 after not prioritising a check-up (and being too 'busy' with work!). Being stuck on a boat at sea for ten weeks in 2020 during the COVID pandemic.	I believe the world needs more heart and humour. It needs more honest conversation, human to human. I do not believe that everyone is a leader. To lead is a choice we must make each day. I believe that deepening our self-awareness is the best gift we can give ourselves and others.	I want to generate warmth with people. I want to do serious work but not take myself too seriously (for example, to share insights but not corporate jargon). I want to be relatable, so that people feel safe to speak up and share.

Once you start drawing out things that are unique and important to you, you will be able to cement and own more about who you are and what you stand for, and what that looks like as actions and behaviours. This will allow you to lead from a deeper place that is true to you.

Over to you.

Your Happy Career Action

What is your own personal USP? Draw up a table similar to mine with three columns and the following headings: Experiences, Thought leadership and Presence. Start populating the columns for yourself. What comes up for you?

Bonus tip: To get the most out of this activity, consider asking a trusted colleague or friend to interview you and fill out the columns while you're talking. You likely say things about yourself that you don't even realise, and someone else actively listening will pick up on them more easily.

The strengths equation you need to build your brand

Said no-one: 'So, Claire, what are your strengths?'

Me: 'I can demolish a wheel of cheese in five seconds, I could kick down a door when Shania Twain sings "Let's go girls!", and when I really laugh at something, I often snort.'

'Right, well, thanks for the honesty.'

Although, in all seriousness, I do consider these things strengths of mine (and they do probably go a long way towards cementing my USP!), they are not quite what I mean when talking about career strengths. To support your USP, you need to back it with strengths and actions you can demonstrate consistently to bring your brand to life in a way that feels authentic to you.

Many experts talk about the importance of playing to your strengths at work, and so they should. Huge value can come from being able to utilise the talents you already have to help deliver outcomes that drive an organisation forward.

This focus on strengths, however, often leads to feedback such as the following:

- 'I'd love to see you leverage your strengths more in this role.'
- 'Just play to your strengths – the rest will follow.'

This feedback isn't wrong, but it isn't overly helpful either. What is often lacking in this conventional advice is the actual 'how to' of playing to your strengths to achieve outcomes for yourself, your team and your organisation. What if you don't know your strengths? Or, what if you aren't sure how the strengths you have can translate into effective outcomes?

The 'play to your strengths' equation is actually made up of four critical parts, and all four need to be in sync in order for you to be effective.

Here's my handy strengths equation for what it takes to play to your strengths well:

Know them + own them + leverage them
+ know the point of reverse impact
= play to your strengths well

Let's delve into each element in this equation.

Know them

To play to your strengths in the workplace and essentially get better results in an easier way, you first must know what your strengths are.

This can be a stumbling block for some people, and I'm often asked how to start determining strengths.

In *Atomic Habits*, James Clear recommends first thinking about the times and scenarios when you feel in 'flow'. To help reflect on this, he asks the following questions:

· What feels like fun to you, but work to others?

· What makes you lose track of time?

· Where do you get greater returns than the average person?

· What comes naturally to you?

In considering your responses, you may want to reflect on past feedback, performance conversations or positive recognition you've received. Can you identify themes in the commentary you've received over the years?

Also consider the kinds of things people regularly come to you for help or advice on. What are you known for in your organisation? What kinds of skills do you use consistently in your day-to-day work?

Getting curious and reflecting on these questions, and then further validating your responses to them by seeking some specific feedback, can help you start to paint a picture of what your unique strengths are.

Own them

Simply knowing what your strengths are isn't enough. You've also got to be able to own them confidently. Why? Because just being regularly told in performance reviews that you are good at something – public speaking, for example – doesn't mean that you believe it, or that you'll utilise it intentionally to help further increase your profile at work if you aren't prepared to own that strength. Knowing that you have certain strengths isn't going to help you if you are unable to state what you do with confidence, or if you don't actually believe in your strengths at all.

I recently had the pleasure of listening to an executive share her career story in a workshop that I was facilitating for a client. This executive talked with conviction and confidence about what she'd learnt her strengths were and how she utilised them every day – and it was such a breath of fresh air to hear! We often worry about stating our strengths out loud because we don't want to come across as 'braggy', and yet we feel quite comfortable about rattling off our weaknesses.

In order to play to your strengths and be sought out for new opportunities at work, you *must* be able to own them – say them out loud to yourself, and to your key stakeholders when needed. An example could be, 'I'm pretty good at facilitating collaborative conversations and getting all the right departments in the room to some clear outcomes. I'd be happy to take the lead on that and report back to you'.

Leverage them

Now that you know what your strengths are and are able to own them with confidence (that is, you can talk proudly and with conviction about why these are your strengths), the next part of the process is to leverage your strengths to get outcomes at work intentionally. This is all about using what you're great at to achieve results with and for other people.

To leverage your strengths effectively, you've got to step back and analyse when and how you can use them. For example, if you've identified that a strength of yours is a strong coaching approach that gets people to open up and feel heard, think about ways to leverage this in different parts of your role. Whereas previously you may have only used this strength during one-on-ones with your team, if you consider ways you could leverage it further, you may uncover many more opportunities. For example, you could deliberately leverage this strength in group meetings with your ability to ask the powerful questions that draw out the right information to move a conversation forward. You could leverage it in a conversation with key stakeholders through paraphrasing and showing them how you're listening to their needs and what's important to them, increasing trust and influence. Knowing how you can practically leverage a strength beyond its most obvious use is key to maximising it.

Know the point of reverse impact

The last part of the formula is also the most important, because it is usually missing in the conversation about playing to your strengths. You need to know your point of reverse impact, or the point when a strength is no longer serving as a strength and is actually hindering you.

As an example of this, I once had a workshop participant who identified that a strength of theirs was being able to distil complex spreadsheet data quickly into stories that people could understand and make better decisions from. Great strength! However, they also realised, and had received feedback to validate this, that their ability to connect the dots in reports more quickly than others was leading them to become visibly frustrated when attempting to support others. Their strength was now actually starting to have a reverse impact and work against them.

Knowing the point of reverse impact of a strength is critical to leading yourself effectively, leading others and getting the results you want.

Table 3 overleaf outlines how these four elements come together for two of my strengths.

Table 3: The four elements of the strengths equation

Know	Own	Leverage	Know the point of reverse impact
Empathy	I've received significant feedback on this over the years through performance reviews, client testimonials and 360 surveys, and I confidently own this as a strength of mine.	This strength can be leveraged through: • actively listening in conversations • asking powerful questions to move conversations forward when people feel stuck • paraphrasing to show people they are heard • ensuring awareness of body language in conversations to demonstrate openness and warmth.	Previously, I have been drawn in too much to someone's challenges and absorbed too much of their emotion, which has impacted my judgement. Now I am more in tune with this, so I can identify when it happens and know how to reframe it.

Know	Own	Leverage	Know the point of reverse impact
Public speaking	It's taken me a little longer to get here and own it, but I am a great public speaker, with multiple touch points of data and validation reinforcing this.	This strength can be leveraged through: • workshops • group coaching • EMCEE events • panel conversations • video recording • webinars • presenting ideas with impact.	At times I have been too enthusiastic and possibly spoken too much, so I regularly ask myself, 'What does success look like for this engagement?' and 'What do listeners need to get out of this?' to ensure I hit the mark.

Turning a weakness into something mediocre takes considerably more time than turning a strength into a superpower. But, here's the thing – playing to your strengths involves more than just deciding to. You must consider all parts of the strengths equation to play to your strengths in a way that sees you yielding the return you want. Know them. Own them. Leverage them. Know the point of reverse impact.

Over to you.

Your Happy Career Action

What are your unique strengths? What do you – and others – consider your career superpowers? How do you tap into all four parts of the strengths equation?

Create a table similar to the one I've provided, and first cement your top ten strengths. Next, work your way through the strengths equation for each one. If you're not sure where to start, seek some feedback from your peers or friends around what they see as your strengths. What do people come to you for advice on? What expertise are you sought out for? These are all great starting points to help you build clarity.

Now that you've got greater clarity on your professional brand, your USP and your strengths, let's talk about the power of leveraging this through social media.

Using social media to your advantage

In my previous corporate HR roles, I saw employees using social media in all the wrong ways – including posting images of themselves doing burnouts in company cars and sculling wine from a cask in the back of a storeroom while on shift. One employee even created a

KKK mask out of company-branded materials, videoed themselves wearing it and then posted it on their socials. (Yep, seriously!)

You might read these examples and think, *Duuuuuuuh, of course that's not using social media for good.* I agree – that would seem obvious, right? Apparently not.

Social media has brought a whole new level of complexity to the question of where the line between work and life is drawn. Although at times I agree this line can be blurry, it is still usually abundantly clear what is right and wrong, and what is going to have a positive impact on your reputation and brand versus what absolutely will not.

Promoting your accomplishments, values, learnings, insights and projects you're excited to be working on via social media is a great way to use it to your advantage. Even though platforms such as LinkedIn are external company tools, they are also platforms that many of your colleagues, peers and senior managers are on – so why would you not use them as positioning or visibility tools in a way that feels right for you?

Where you can go wrong, however, is to forget that a public platform is just that – *public*. Everything you put online will enhance or detract from your brand. If you want to build a career more on happy rather than hustle, knowing how you want to be portrayed and then living it through the way you show up everywhere, including online, is such a key part of that.

This doesn't mean you need to be stiff, sterile and only use corporate speak. (Yawn.) Your brand is a human being (you!), so showcase the many parts of you. For example, clients of mine will see a Claire who is passionate about career and leadership development, but they will also see a Claire who loves to travel, has a sausage dog called Kransky, loves a good meal with friends and a hearty conversation, and loves a good laugh about life.

These things enhance my brand rather than detract from it. If anything, sharing these aspects of myself creates deeper connections for people to have with my brand because they see more than just one dimension of it.

The same is true for you.

When deciding how to use social media (and I mean all types of social media) to your advantage, ask yourself the following:

- Is what I'm posting aligned with what I want to be known for?
- Is it consistent with the behaviours and actions I demonstrate at work?
- If my key stakeholders saw this and then started a conversation with me about it, would I be comfortable and proud to talk about that?

Your brand and, therefore, your reputation are so important for your career. Your brand will grow and evolve as you grow and evolve. Nurture it, protect it, and be intentional and deliberate about how you share it with the world.

Key takeaways

Here's the second element in a nutshell:

- Your brand is your reputation inside and outside your organisation. It is created in the micro-moments, not just in your one-off actions. Consistency is key.
- Every single one of us has our own USP, made up of our experiences, values and beliefs, and the presence that we bring to those in our orbit. Do you know yours?

- Playing to your strengths and being seen and valued at work means using all four elements of the strengths equation – knowing, owning, leveraging and being aware of the reverse point of impact of each of your strengths.

- Social media can enhance and detract from your brand and reputation. Be intentional about what you share and why. Is it something you'd be proud to talk about if asked about it by a leader at your organisation?

Chapter 5

Element three: Accelerating growth through relationships

Imagine this scenario for a moment. You have two colleagues who both need your help or assistance at the same time. You are only one person, so you can only help one at a time. Who do you go to first?

Let's assume that neither is asking about an emergency situation. (Hopefully, if one was, you'd prioritise the emergency!) Let's also assume that neither is your direct manager or someone from the executive team, because I'm sure you'd also likely prioritise them. Nope, these are just two peers asking you to give up some of your resources (aka time!) to help them with something they need.

I guarantee you that you will almost always go first to help the person you have greater rapport with, connection with, or trust in. It is likely that they've invested time in getting to know you too, or they may have even helped you before. Whether you like it or not, this is the way humans are wired. We are a relationship-focused bunch.

In this third element of my five-part career framework, I look at why relationships really are the key to your success (however you've defined it). More importantly, I also outline the 'how to' of nurturing and sustaining relationships, so you not only get outcomes but also feel good about it. I outline why influence is the new power supply in your organisation, and I help you take a step back to think about the actions you need to take to invest in your own networks.

Why relationships really are your key to success

We all have limited resources. Therefore, you have to make decisions daily on how to use your resources to maximise returns, hopefully for the best return for you and for your peer, team or organisation – ideally, for everyone involved.

I mentioned Carla Harris in chapter 1 in relation to the concepts of relationship and performance currency. Harris also has a famous TED Talk – 'How to find the person who can help you get ahead at work' – where she digs into relationship currency as being what you generate via the investments that you make in the people in your environment.

Harris states that at a minimum you need to have a relationship with every 'seat that touches your seat'. This means, at an absolute base level, you should be focusing on the strength of your relationship with every person you need to be able to do your job effectively. If the only person in your environment who knows you and knows you are doing a great job is your boss, you may find it difficult to ascend, because that person may leave the organisation or lose their seat at the table one day.

Let me just pause here. If reading about relationships as currency makes you feel icky, I get it. I felt that way too when the concept was first introduced to me. I thought 'relationship currency' meant we were supposed to think about the people in our orbit as a series of jars that we put money into and took money out of. Each positive interaction or experience, such as a small favour or meaningful exchange, increased the amount in the jar. The fuller the jar, the stronger the relationship – and the more you could withdraw as needed. It felt very transactional.

Ewww... Are people just coin jars now? Yes, and no.

Because then I realised this: this concept was playing out with me and around me whether I liked it or not every single day. And now that I knew about it, I could see it everywhere. The only choice I had to make now was *how* I wanted to engage with it.

The same is true for you. The first question to honestly ask yourself is, 'What value am I currently placing on the relationships I have with people at work?' And then, secondly, 'What consistent actions do I take to demonstrate this?'

If you work with the attitude of 'Can't I just do my job in peace?', you are likely already on the back foot. In organisations, things get done *with* and *through* people. This is true whether you formally lead a team or not.

Don't be a 'dag', though

I previously worked with two people who were often referred to within the business as 'dags'. If you're unfamiliar with the Australian rural vernacular, the *Oxford Dictionary of English Idioms* defines dags as 'the excreta-clotted lumps of wool at the rear end of a sheep, which, in heavily fouled animals, rattle as they run'. Firstly, sorry if you're eating as you read this. Secondly, how on earth is this relevant? Let me explain.

These people were dags in the sense that they came across as disingenuously clingy with certain people in the business who they deemed important or who held status, but totally excluded and isolated all others. Such an approach is the opposite of Harris's concept of relationship currency and the importance of having a relationship with every seat that touches your seat, which advocates seeing the value in relationships with more people than just the CEO or other key power brokers in an organisation.

To take Harris's concept further, though, it is also critical to consider the 'future potential value' of relationships. People may not be in influential or decision-making positions at this very moment, but they may be in the future. And this is where my dag colleagues went very, very wrong. They treated those in senior roles a certain way, but spoke to the receptionist, the customer service team and anyone they deemed 'less important' a totally different way. They were the kind of peers who look around you when they talk to you in case they spot a better opportunity. They were the kind of peers who would leave the receptionist a note asking them to unpack and prepare materials for them, and then walk into a room with the leadership team saying how long they'd spent preparing those same materials.

These people had forgotten (or maybe just undervalued) the concept that our reputations and relationships are built through our actions, not our words, and the actions we demonstrate day to day, not just when we are 'on show'. Equally as important, relationships are built fundamentally on trust.

Fast-forward two years, and several hierarchical changes had occurred in this organisation. Different people were now in positions of influence and 'power', and all of sudden our 'dags', who had not invested sincerely in any other relationships than the sheep they had been desperately clinging to, were now left out to dry (or drop, if I can continue the sheep analogy). They were now left without influence, without a strong and positive brand, and without much opportunity.

Relationships matter.

Build trust the right way

When I was living in Melbourne, I had the best hairdresser I have ever had. His name was Ross and he was fabulous. I would wait months for an appointment with Ross, and I wouldn't let anyone else touch my hair because they just weren't Ross. It got to the point where I wouldn't even need to discuss what he would do to my hair at each salon visit – I just let him go. And I was able to do that because I trusted him to deliver. I trusted him to have my back (or my hair, in this case).

My current hairdresser is fine, but they aren't Ross. Every time I go, we still need to have a clear consultation about what needs to happen, and I still sit there nervously *hoping* it goes the way I want it to.

What did Ross do differently to inspire such strong levels of trust? He asked the right questions. He really listened to my responses, and usually played them back to me to demonstrate he'd heard me. He was genuinely interested in understanding what I valued and what was important to me. And then he took all that on board, added his own lens and expertise, and delivered.

The same skills are required inside organisations, and they are what separate the 'fine' relationships from the 'fabulous'.

Building trust isn't just on one person, however.

It is easy to say that trust in organisations starts and stops with the leader. Yes, a leader supports the creation of a culture and demonstrates the acceptable behaviour within a business or a team through the way they recognise and reward. However, I also believe that each individual within the organisation has a responsibility to themselves and their colleagues for the part they play in the relationships they cultivate. The depth and sincerity of these relationships is up to you, the individual, not your leader. Trust must be nurtured and consistently worked on.

In *The Trusted Advisor*, professional advisors David Maister, Charles Green and Robert Galford explore the concept of how to increase your trust quotient for better and more effective relationships. The book references four key components of trusting relationships. Three are enhancers of trust, and one is a potential detractor of trust.

Here are the four key components of trusting relationships and how they work together:

1. **Credibility.** Can people believe in and trust what you're saying? How do you show people?

2. **Reliability.** How dependable are you? Can people count on you, and do you have people's backs? Note that reliability doesn't mean perfection.

3. **Intimacy.** How connected are people with you? Do they feel they know you, and so can trust you, or are you completely emotionally detached?

4. **Self-orientation.** How obvious is your own personal focus, self-interest or agenda? Showing too much self-focus or an obvious agenda can detract from trust, if it is not supplemented consistently and intentionally by credibility, reliability and intimacy.

So, back to my hairdresser. Here's how Ross scored on the trust equation:

-   **Credibility.** Every time I was in the salon, it was clear to me that Ross knew best. This was shown most strongly by the number of other hairdressers who would come up to him with questions, wanting his opinion or his expertise. He was clearly knowledgeable, which made me further invested in what he had to say.

- **Reliability.** The more engagements I had with Ross, and the more he continued to deliver on what he said he would (to give me great hair!), the deeper the level of faith and trust I had in him. The link between what he committed to doing and then what he actually did was strong, and therefore reliable.

- **Intimacy.** In the earlier stages of our relationship, Ross would always ask questions about what was important to me, what success looked like to me (for my hair), and what I valued. He connected with me through a good questioning technique but then, more importantly, listened to the answers. This allowed me to feel heard, seen and understood. Ross also shared a bit about himself, which further built relationship depth and trust over time. He also somehow managed to remember almost everything I shared with him about myself, too.

- **Self-orientation.** Maybe this is just a 'me' issue, but I hate hairdressers pushing products onto me, especially when the product isn't relevant to any treatment I am having, or when the suggestion comes too early in the consultation. It's self-serving, given they are likely getting commissions off the sale, and it can detract from the sincerity of the relationship when done prematurely. Ross did not do this until some time into our partnership. He waited until he understood more about me and was able to demonstrate some results, and then made some suggestions around what might enhance those results further. I accepted his suggestions immediately.

Okay, let's get beyond hair.

As I hope you're starting to see, effective relationship-building and trust is an art, a science, and a necessary part of building a career more on happy and less on hustle.

Steps for building trust

Wondering how to cultivate greater trust with your peers? With any action you take to work on your relationships, consistency and sincerity are key, as is aligning with the trust equation:

$$Trust = (Credibility + Reliability + Intimacy) - Self\text{-}orientation$$

Here are some practical tips to help you do just that:

- **Don't be a dag.** Treat everyone with the same level of respect, regardless of their status or position in the organisation. If your colleagues see you speak one way to an executive leader and then another way to the receptionist or cleaner, you'll come across as non-genuine, out for yourself and, ultimately, untrustworthy.

- **More serve, less self-serve.** Instead of only considering the value of a relationship based on what you need from someone now, consider what you can give in return. What support can you offer? What connections can you make to assist someone? How can you listen to someone to allow them to feel heard, seen and valued? Reciprocity is a powerful building block of relationships.

- **Seek to understand before you offer.** Often we listen purely to respond, instead of listening to hear or understand people. Take the time to understand where others are coming from by actively listening to what they are saying before you feel the need to offer advice or tell them something about your own situation. How will you know you've done this? You'll be in a real two-way dialogue, instead of just two people relaying their thoughts to one another without any connection or flow in the conversation.

- **Small gestures show that you think of others.** Small and consistent gestures can make a huge difference when building authentic working relationships. Such gestures could include grabbing an extra coffee on the way to work for someone, dropping someone's mail at their desk, saying good morning when you arrive each day, and asking someone how they are *and* stopping to listen to their answer.

- **Walk the talk and talk the walk.** Consider how your body language aligns with what you say. Saying to someone you really value their opinion and perspective, but then staring at your computer screen while they share it with you, sends a mixed message and equates to a big 'say versus do' gap that is not conducive to building trust.

- **Be a human being, not just a human doing.** Share something of yourself with people and take a genuine interest in others in return. Being vulnerable and honest with people about who you are, how you're feeling and your past experiences is a great way to break down barriers and build more depth into your relationships.

Over to you. How can you work on your relationships?

Your Happy Career Action

Write a list of all of the key people who you need to have an effective relationship with in order to do your job well and progress in your career. Next, review and assess each of those relationships against the trust equation.

Following that, consider these reflection questions against each of the people you captured on your list:

- How are they doing, really? Do you know?

- What do you know about that person versus what they know about you?

- What's happening in their working world at the moment? What challenges are they facing? What is important to them? What priorities do they have?

- When you spend time with this person, are you often in one-way conversations (that is, you talking at them), or are you engaged in true dialogue and listening to each other to understand?

- How open are you to this person's opinions and perspectives? How do you demonstrate this when you engage with them?

When it comes to a career built more on happy and less on hustle, having strong and effective relationships throughout your entire career is key. Your goal is to be in a position where you have an army of people who have your back, and you have theirs in return. Feeling connected in this way not only feels good but also goes a long way to building deeper influence. And we all want a little more influence, don't we?

Influence – the new power supply in workplaces

'I'd really be keen to know what Cindy's take on that is', said a senior leader in the business I was in at the time. *Interesting*, I thought to myself. Cindy wasn't a subject matter expert in the area being discussed. Cindy also wasn't hierarchically senior enough to particularly warrant involvement from a decision-making perspective. Do you know what Cindy had, though? Influence. By the truckload.

Influence is what enables you to get your opinions, needs, recommendations and requirements across the line with greater ease, because people are more open to listening to what you have to say. In order for people to be more open to what you have to say, though, you also need to have a relationship with them.

Cindy had positioned herself inside the organisation as someone who had their finger on the pulse – the real pulse. She'd well and truly worked on the trust equation with multiple stakeholders and was seeing a serious return on that investment. Cindy knew what the prevailing sentiment in the organisation was. She knew the conversations that were happening behind closed doors. She knew the said and the unsaid, and what it all meant. People *wanted* to listen to Cindy. On that basis alone, she had influence.

Acknowledging that influence is the new power supply inside the complex, multi-layered organisations that we now work in is an important place to start. Add to that hybrid or fully remote working, and the need for influence becomes even more critical to getting outcomes in a way that doesn't only come from hustle.

Traditionally, power inside organisations was only given to the few who sat at the pointy end of the org-chart triangle; however, this is no longer the only power supply. Power runs deep and wide through an organisation. And again, unsurprisingly, it is often built on the relationships that you have, hold and nurture.

Using influence as a magnet, not a firehose

When you think of influence in the context of work, you might think about it through the lens of, 'Who do I need to influence to get them to spend some of their resources on my needs?' 'Resources' here might be time, budget, headcount, connections, decision-making authority, or even their personal power and advocacy. Whatever resource you're hoping to acquire from someone, your strategy might be simply to tell them what you need from them and when you need it.

However, using this strategy means you forget to share two critical aspects:

1. Why you need it
2. Why they should care – what's in it for them?

When it comes to building genuine influence, that's just what you need to do – influence, not impose. In order to influence effectively, you need to pull people into your vision, rather than push it upon them.

That's right – less push, more pull.

How can you draw people into your orbit because they *want* to hear or understand your perspective, your recommendation or idea, instead of having it pushed down their throat? You enable others to feel seen, heard and understood. People want to work with people who they feel 'get' them – people who understand them and know their pain, frustrations and challenges.

Think about it. When you vote in an election, you vote for the candidate who you believe best understands and represents your interests. You vote for the candidate who most closely appears to understand what is important to you. When you walk in to cast your vote, volunteers for different political parties practically throw leaflets at you, telling you why their party is the best. And yet, rarely if ever do they ask first what is important to you. At that point, it's likely too late anyway. The influence opportunities have already occurred well before you wait in the queue to cast your vote, grab your democracy sausage and hightail it out of there.

Push mode is a last resort.

Influence happens in the mundane moments

You are building personal influence inside your organisation and in your career overall well before you ever walk into a room to pitch an idea, present a thought or make a request. Your influence-building is happening in every moment, but particularly in the mundane ones. I'm talking here about the moments when you're having conversations with people outside the formal meeting rooms.

Think back to the story I shared in chapter 1, about the time I'd spent days creating a strategy PowerPoint to present to my leadership team, ensuring it was polished, beautifully presented and included all the right buzzwords.

I'd put everything on the conversation that was going to happen 'in the room'. I was ready to push my thoughts *onto* people. I'd put little to no time or focus on the importance of the conversations that happened outside of the room – that is, the 'pull' part. I'd ignored the temperature-check conversations I should have been having along the way. These were the conversations that would have really told me what the challenges, priorities and frustrations of my stakeholders were, so that I could play that back in the room alongside my recommendations to help solve them.

I had put all my chips down on the table in the room, but I hadn't assessed the players around me, what hands they might have, or what cards they were searching for to complement their current hands.

Relationships and influence take work

As I have said, all human beings want to feel heard, seen, valued and understood. A critical way you can do that is by engaging genuinely with people – by asking insightful questions, playing back what you've heard to show you were listening and to confirm alignment, and showing you are engaged through your body language. Most importantly, you can genuinely engage with people by being sincerely curious.

Instead of going from meeting to meeting, task to task, hustling away and feeling like you're not actually moving forward, I invite you to stop, step back, and ask yourself these questions:

- What do I really know about what my stakeholders value?
- Who do I need to be more curious about? How can I show that I'm curious?

In what has now become one of the most famous statements in the world of professional development and leadership, leadership expert Simon Sinek said, 'People don't buy what you do; they buy why you do it'. So, why should your stakeholders buy what you're selling – what's really in it for them? When you push less and pull more through understanding your stakeholder needs, priorities and resistance, you'll be better positioned to have a career built less on hustle and more on happy.

Close the loop – always

A coaching client of mine – let's call her Danielle – had an epiphany recently. Danielle was so excited by the time she had just spent with a senior executive inside her organisation. That executive had given Danielle an hour of her time in a mentoring capacity outside any kind of formal program, just to answer questions Danielle had about the executive's career lessons, learnings, current business challenges and priorities, and about how to grow inside the organisation.

Danielle told me she felt thrilled by this conversation and was energised and motivated to continue growing and learning within the company. When I then asked her how she had closed the loop, I received this response.

…

Crickets.

…

'What do you mean, close the loop?' she eventually said. So I asked her how she closed the loop following her conversation to ensure the executive knew she was grateful for their time and expertise, and to ensure she left the door open for a future conversation. Danielle's response to this was, 'I haven't said or done anything since my catch-up with them'.

This is not at all uncommon. When someone invests their time to understand your needs, your challenges, and your goals or aspirations, they are saying yes to you and no to something else. Time is a currency, and when someone is giving it to you, it is important to always prepare, and to respect it.

Close the loop, always.

Closing the loop with a follow-up note on your key takeaways, the actions you're committing to or even just gratitude showcases professionalism and respect. It also increases the likelihood of that person being open to sharing their time (currency) again with you and talking about it with others.

This approach can be used beyond just one-on-one conversations too. Perhaps a colleague of yours spoke at a town hall or a full company meeting. Closing the loop with them sincerely by sending a note about what you learnt from them or what resonated is a great way to continue to build your relationships and influence within your organisation – and not to mention a great way to make someone else feel good and support your network.

When these 'closing the loop' gestures are made consistently (and with genuine intent), they become a building block for a deeper relationship and a key part of increasing your visibility inside the organisation. If any part of you still feels icky about this, or that it is a waste of time, I suggest you go back to element one and particularly consider the sections on mindset and career beliefs. Spend some time there, and then let's catch up again.

Over to you.

Networking doesn't have to be soul-sucking

I hate 'small talk' – seriously. But I don't hate it for the reasons that you might think. I'm actually quite good at it. I hate it because I crave the real stuff – the deep stuff. And I am quite comfortable to dive straight into conversations about the meaning of life with someone that I've just met. In fact, I'll choose that any day over having 25 conversations about the weather, and whether it's a 'dry heat' we're currently in or a 'humid heat'.

Spoon. Eyeballs. Now. Please.

But here is what I also have learnt about 'small talk'. Small talk builds big talk. And small talk is only as small as you choose to make it. The broader your network, the fewer repetitive conversations you have to hear and be part of.

Are you playing a game of Jenga?

When you consider your networks, do you also consider how broad they are? Are they diverse and built from relationships with people from many different areas of life? Or are they small, insular and comfortable, grown from the people you're immediately surrounded with in your current position and organisation who think similarly to you?

I recently facilitated a women in leadership program in collaboration with former politician Julie Bishop. In the program, Julie used the analogy of a tower versus a pyramid in the context of building strategic networks and effective relationships. I thought this was a great way to look at it. A tower can be tall but is relatively thin. Removing one or two pieces can be enough for the whole thing to tumble. A tower has little breadth of footprint and is reasonably insular in structure. A pyramid, on the other hand, is built on broader foundations, arguably making it stronger and better supported overall and for the longer term.

You want your network to look more like a pyramid than a tower. Cultivating and sincerely nurturing a broad network of people from all layers of your organisation, and from outside your organisation, with different roles, backgrounds and ways of thinking is the best way to ensure you've got a strong network that you can both contribute to and leverage for the long game.

Networks are like a blue-chip stock

'I'm just too busy working to go to networking events – I don't have time for them.' Oh, if I had a dollar for every time I heard this statement!

Firstly, networking is working.

Secondly, when you consider networking, you likely picture awkwardly standing at a networking sundowner hoping you might meet someone new, but also secretly hoping that the fire emergency alarm goes off and you can go home.

Don't get me wrong – meeting new people is great and is an important part of growth. But what about the people you've also already met along the way? I'm talking about the people you've worked with in past organisations, as well as the people from courses you've been on, sports you've played, events you've been to, and friends of friends you've met. After you met them and said, 'Let's keep in touch', what happened?

Nurturing relationships you already have is far easier than continuing to go out and build more but then not cultivating them. The latter option is like endlessly throwing seeds into a field and then not watering them.

We often neglect our existing relationships, though, because we may not see an immediate return on the relationship. Maybe the person you've just met is not in a position of 'power' right now, or maybe they don't work for the company you want to get into, but that's a short-sighted view.

People in your network need to be treated like blue-chip stocks. You're with them for the long haul. They may not skyrocket overnight like a specky stock can (although I have seen this happen many times too!), but they will consistently deliver a return if you hold onto them – time after time, and year after year.

Maintaining your networks both internally and externally to your organisation, and for the long haul, is one of the biggest investments you can make for yourself and for your career.

When is the best time to start? Yesterday.

Building your board of career advisors

Opinions are everywhere – some are helpful, and some are not. When it comes to building a career based more on happy and less on hustle or hope, it is important that you know exactly whose opinions and advice you should listen to. This will also change over the course of your career.

Building a robust board of career advisors is akin to assembling a personal advisory dream team. Each member plays a distinct role in guiding, supporting and advocating for your professional growth and success. Six key roles are essential within this board for your career success, but these roles don't necessarily need to be filled by six different people. Having between three and six trusted people from diverse backgrounds is key.

Over my career, various individuals have played these roles and had a huge impact on my career (and my life!), just as I too have played these roles for others in return. Sometimes, the role has been formalised, and other times the role has formed more organically. What's important is that your board is intentional, diverse and strategic.

Here are the roles you should consider filling in your career dream team:

- **Coach.** This is a person who can challenge your thinking and provoke new ways of working for you. A coach isn't there to tell you what to do; instead, they are there to prompt you to think for yourself. They'll challenge you to think differently and broaden your perspective.

- **Mentor.** This is a person who has been, or is, where you want to go, and can therefore share their wisdom and experiences with you for you to learn from. They serve as sounding boards for ideas, offer perspective during challenging situations, and help you capitalise on opportunities for growth.

- **Sponsor.** A sponsor is a powerful advocate who actively promotes your career advancement within their network and organisation. They champion your talents, recommend you for promotions or high-profile projects, and actively endorse your capabilities to other key decision-makers. Having a sponsor can significantly accelerate your career progression by opening doors that might otherwise remain closed to you. A critical point to consider here is that your sponsor must be in the rooms where decisions are being made in order to be impactful to your career.

- **Confidant.** This is someone in your professional world who you completely trust and can 'offload' to as needed. Importantly, though, your confidant should also be someone who is future-focused and constructive, not someone who will keep you stuck or in a toxic headspace – that isn't what a happy career is built on!

- **Connector.** As already established, a strong network is an essential aspect of career advancement, and a connector plays a pivotal role in supporting you to expand yours. They are skilled at making introductions, facilitating meaningful connections and creating opportunities for collaboration. Connectors help you broaden your circle, access new resources and forge relationships with individuals who can contribute to your career growth, or who you may be able to contribute to in return.

What vacancies do you currently have on your board of career advisors? Ask yourself the following when assessing who might be a valuable addition to your board:

- Have I chosen people who have already reached a goal that I have for myself, who have inspired me, or who have helped others realise their potential?
- Have I chosen people from diverse backgrounds?
- Have I chosen people who will challenge me to think and act critically?
- Have the people I've chosen been supportive of me and my goals in the past?
- Have I chosen people who will benefit from this relationship too?

Over to you. Who's on your career dream team?

Your Happy Career Action

Once you have identified the members you may want for your career dream team, you now need to go back to the fundamentals of what makes a great relationship with someone. Ask yourself honestly, 'Do I have these things in place with these people?' What level of relationship currency do you think you have? If it's strong, great – you might be ready for a conversation with them about how you'd love to connect with them more regularly as your mentor or coach if they'd be open to it.

If you don't have strong relationship currency, or you aren't sure, your next step is to start putting some small and consistent actions in place to build that relationship with them more deeply first, or to increase your visibility.

To round out this third element of my five-part career framework, remember that relationships are worth 50 per cent of your career currency. If you want a long-term, sustainable career built more on happy and less on hustle, you need to prioritise building strong, effective and powerful networks, internally and externally, for the long game. Not only does your working world become more enjoyable as a result, but results also come more easily.

Key takeaways

Here's the third element in a nutshell:

- Relationships make up 50 per cent of your career currency framework. Not investing in them consistently and deliberately means that you are limiting your potential for growth in your career.

- Building trust is fundamental to effective relationships. There are three critical trust enhancers (credibility, reliability and intimacy) and one potential trust detractor (self-orientation).

- Influence is built by the way you draw people into your world, and not by the way you push your needs onto them. You can draw people in by taking a genuine interest in who they are and how they see things.

- Your networks need to be nurtured across the course of your entire career, not just when you need something from someone. It is also far easier to nurture relationships you already have, rather than continue to plant new seeds that you then don't water.

- Building a board of career advisors is an essential ingredient to building a successful career, and is made up of a number of key roles.

Chapter 6

Element four: Building your performance currency

Now that you know just how critical a strong level of relationship currency is for you to truly have a happy career, you can turn your attention to the fourth element in my five-part career framework – the concept of performance currency.

Monkey see, monkey do – the same is true for you

Think back to your first corporate job. What was it like? What kinds of behaviours did you observe? What behaviours were rewarded? Perhaps you witnessed behaviours, traits and ways of working inside the organisation that you then adopted (perhaps even unconsciously). This is particularly common early on in people's careers because they assume that is what is needed to get ahead and succeed.

I never saw it at the time because I was too early in my career to realise, but my first job was entirely a presenteeism culture.

A 'presenteeism' culture is one in which being present at work is more important than being productive at work. In my first job, the way you generated currency was to just be visible at your desk – even if you did nothing at it.

I started my first full-time corporate job when I was 19 (while also studying at university full-time). The role was with a fairly small business, and my job responsibilities were varied (as they often are in a small business). I was responsible for anything from marketing activities and client liaison to communications and the odd voice-over artistry. (That's a story for another day!)

I recall one day getting to work five minutes late, and my boss was standing at the door looking at his watch. The same thing would happen at the end of the day if anyone dared to leave even a moment before 5 pm. And yet, we could sit at our desks all day scrolling social media, or googling cute puppies, and he wouldn't say a thing. This was my introduction to corporate life. Be present. Be physically visible. Stretch your work to fit the day. In hindsight, this was never going to align with my career values and my personal definition of success – basically, it made me want to bang my head against a wall.

At the time, I had no understanding of the concept of performance currency, but if I had, it would have allowed me to maximise my contribution in a more effective way, and channel my efforts, expertise and enthusiasm in ways that meant more happy! Because let me tell you this:

Real performance currency is more than smiling at your boss while watching cute puppy videos on TikTok.

Luckily for me, I learnt quickly what was actually important to demonstrate real performance currency, and after moving to my second full-time role in a much larger organisation, I was given two promotions in an 18-month period and so many development opportunities. I attribute those to me leveraging the full suite of tools I teach you in this book. In particular, though, at that early stage in my career, I attribute those promotions to the performance currency strategies I share with you in this chapter.

Performance currency is the way in which you demonstrate what you know and deliver on the things you're accountable for, and more. Your managers and workmates assume you are able to do your job; however, to really elevate the worth of your currency, your key stakeholders need to see your ability to exceed expectations and demonstrate enough potential that they want to invest in you for the long term.

The five levers I walk you through in this chapter will see your performance currency skyrocket if you do them consistently. When done consistently and correctly, these do not equate to more work – they just equate to better outcomes.

The five levers are as follows:

1. Speaking the language of the business
2. Getting beyond what you know – communicating like a pro
3. Learning to manage conflict well
4. Mastering the full menu of feedback – get, give and receive it well
5. Using strategic self-promotion.

By now you're hopefully seeing how the message of this book was never about working less to make you happy (unless, of course, that is a deliberate choice you make as part of your definition of career success), but rather, it is about working in a way that channels your effort and expertise to get results and increase your enthusiasm at the same time.

So, let's build that performance currency.

Speaking the language of the business

When people talk about the work they do to demonstrate their contribution to their manager, team or organisation, they often talk about *inputs*. This means they use statements like the following:

- 'I've been working really hard.'
- 'I had a huge week of meetings this week and then caught up with *XYZ*, which took up most of my time on Thursday.'
- 'The team and I had to do a fair bit of overtime this week, but we dug in and got it done.'

These statements aren't bad – it's clear anyone making them believes they're busy. However, statements like these don't indicate what you're achieving or delivering by being so busy. When you communicate to your manager or any of your key stakeholders with the desire to increase your performance currency, you need to talk about *outputs* and *outcomes*, not just inputs.

For example, consider the following statement: 'We have been able to onboard ten new starters three weeks ahead of project schedule, which has meant they've hit the road earlier than anticipated, and the sales team have confirmed that's brought in an additional $250k revenue for the project. This means we're now ahead on the project and in revenue delivery.'

Doesn't that sound far more impactful than 'the team is working really hard and we've got lots on'?

To think more deeply about outputs and outcomes, think about your organisation and your purpose in it. What do you know about the business you're in? What do you know about what the organisation is there to achieve? And how does what you do each day enable those company goals to be brought to life? If you're reading this and thinking, *My role doesn't do anything to help the company with its financial goals*, I assure you that you are wrong. Every role in an organisation contributes to outcomes. If it doesn't, then that's a bigger conversation.

Say you are a customer service representative. This means you are on the front line of your organisation, serving as the first point of contact for customers. You are also the bridge between customers and the company, fostering positive relationships and promoting loyalty. Loyalty equates to sales, and sales support growth. You act as a key data source for the customer to the company as well, providing valuable insights on what is important to the customer and, in turn, supporting the organisation in its decision-making.

Every role has a purpose; you need to be clear on yours.

Once you're clear on your role's purpose, you need to be able to consistently link this purpose to the outcomes you are helping to deliver for your team, department or organisation. This will help you demonstrate you are a high-potential employee who 'gets business', instead of one who works hard but doesn't have strong business acumen. By the way, this doesn't mean you need to be an expert accountant, but you do need to understand how the business you're in measures success, and by what metrics.

Over to you. How can you take what you know about your organisation to help increase your performance currency in it?

Your Happy Career Action

Grab a blank piece of paper and write down everything you know about what is important to the organisation you work for right now:

- What is it there to achieve?
- What is its mission?
- What are its values?
- Who are its competitors?

- What are its financial or strategic goals?
- What are some of the things that might keep your CEO or manager up at night right now? What would some of their challenges be?

Hint: you should be able to find most of this stuff on your organisation's website, intranet or company reports.

If you find you struggle with this activity, that's okay – we all start somewhere. Reach out to someone in the organisation and start asking them some of these questions to help you learn (and grow your relationship currency at the same time!). And for some bonus stakeholder questions to help you get started at increasing your business acumen, follow the prompts via the QR code at the back of this book.

Getting beyond what you know – communicating like a pro

Speaking the language of the business helps you take what you know and what you do, and then turn it into something that shows its positive impact on others as well. Doing this well means communication is key. But first, let's have a quick look at what not to do...

'I'm getting really frustrated because it feels like no-one is listening to me.' These were the exact words a colleague said to me one day when they were almost at their wits' end with a project we were working on. Were they wrong in their feelings? Absolutely not. Were they fully justified in their feelings? Also not.

Here's the thing when it comes to communicating like a pro: it doesn't matter how good *you* think you are at it. It only matters how good your *stakeholders* think you are at it. My colleague had done all the 'right' things. She had written out what needed to happen. In fact, she had spent many hours on a lengthy document that she had circulated for everyone to read capturing all of her thoughts, requirements and deadlines. And yet, it didn't work. The wrong actions were taken. The wrong areas were still being focused on, and the wrong outcomes were still being produced, all of which ultimately led to her frustration.

Let me be clear here. Your ability to reduce your hustle lies heavily in your ability to communicate in the way the key people in your working world need to hear information to understand it. To put it another way:

No-one cares about the way you want to communicate it.

I said what I said – sorry, not sorry.

But seriously, in order to bring people on the journey with you, and for them to take the action you need them to take, you need to communicate things in a way that is meaningful to them, not just meaningful to you. Does this (and your life) become infinitely easier when you know your stakeholders well enough to know what is important to them and how they like to communicate? Heck yes – so if you skipped element three on relationships (chapter 5), I suggest you go back now and read it.

Getting your message across effectively

In *The Organized Mind: Thinking straight in the age of information overload*, neuroscientist Daniel Levitin talks about the processing capacity of the conscious mind, estimated at 120 bits per second. That bandwidth is the speed limit for the traffic of information we can pay conscious attention to at any one time. According to Levitin, in order to understand one person speaking to us, we need to process 60 bits of information per second. Our processing limit of 120 bits per second means we can barely understand two people talking to us at the same time, let alone three or more! Throw in our own intrusive thoughts and our ability to listen reduces even more. As Levitin says, it's no wonder the world is filled with so much misunderstanding and confusion.

When you consider how much information we all are processing every day, both consciously and unconsciously, it becomes clear why being able to get your point across concisely and effectively is so damn important.

Effective communication occurs when you deliver a message, it is received and understood the way you intended it to be, *and* the right action is then taken. And, yet, most of the time we say things like, 'Arrgh, I told them what I needed. I don't get why they didn't do it'. They may have done it – they just did it in the way that they understood it.

It's important to remember here that your lens looks a little different. And because the lens through which you view the world is not the same as the person's next to you, when you communicate your what and why based just on how *you* see things and not on how your *stakeholders* see things, you can often wind up frustrated, frazzled and feeling like you're working really hard with no return. You're hustling. So, how do you increase the chances of being heard and understood?

Completing a stakeholder communication audit

Reflect on each one of your core stakeholders and how they communicate. Are they more detail-oriented, and like to review reports themselves and then drill into the detail? Or, are they more of a visionary communicator – they want to be sold to and brought into the vision of success, but they tune out when it gets to the nitty-gritty details?

What you're considering here is how best to engage your stakeholders and get them on board with an idea or a recommendation. Would they prefer to see evidence through data, or is storytelling more likely to engage them? Would they need a demonstration to bring something to life, or would they prefer to join you on a project and have a go at doing it themselves to really understand the value or importance of something?

Meeting them in their lane

Intentionally considering how your stakeholders themselves communicate – and what their priorities and resistance might be – and *then* putting your pitch together based on this information will likely enhance your chance of being heard. Your content is still the same, but the way you deliver it has changed.

In *Lead the Room: Communicate a message that counts in moments that matter*, my good friend Shane Hatton says, 'People don't just listen *because* you speak. They listen when you give them a *reason* to'. If you cannot learn the language of the room – that is, the political landscape, the priorities, the emotion and any resistance in it – you will always struggle to influence it and impact it.

Communicating well is performance currency–building in action, and sometimes it may also mean navigating conflict. Let's look at that now.

Learning to manage conflict well

Conflict exists in every organisation on the planet. It is an inevitable part of your career (and your life!), so learning to manage it well presents a huge opportunity for you to build your performance currency. Perhaps you're wondering something along the lines of, *How is embracing conflict going to increase my performance currency, or give me a happy career?* Fair question. Luckily for you, I'm here to answer it.

Having an ability to navigate conflict well means you're able to get results more easily and keep your relationships in place, all with less hustle. And the good news is that learning how to deal with conflict well often means utilising the same skills and tools you need to tap into when you want to influence, when you want to connect with others, and when you want to negotiate. Basically, these are human skills. So, you're already well on your way there.

At its core, conflict is a difference of opinion between two or more people. The way it is dealt with is usually what makes us the most nervous. I want to share with you some ways that you can learn to deal with conflict well, even if you hate the idea of it.

Know your default conflict style

When it comes to conflict, knowing yourself is key. The Thomas-Kilmann Model of conflict resolution outlines five conflict styles based on how assertive and cooperative an individual is:

1. **Competitive.** You view conflict as something to 'win', often with little or no concern for the other party's needs.
2. **Compromising.** You view conflict as something where all parties should have to sacrifice something to progress.
3. **Collaborating.** You view conflict as an opportunity to find solutions that satisfy both you and the other party.
4. **Avoiding.** You view conflict as something to be avoided at all costs because it is uncomfortable and you feel it doesn't end well.
5. **Accommodating.** You often put the needs of the other party before your own needs in an attempt to keep things smooth and preserve the relationship and your comfort.

The Thomas-Kilmann Model then positions these styles based on their levels of assertiveness and cooperativeness, as shown in figure 4.

Figure 4: The Thomas-Kilmann Model

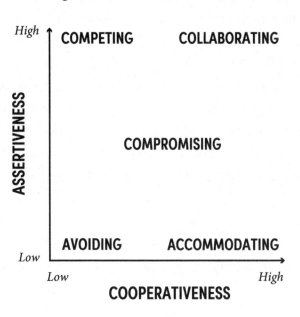

While you have the capacity to navigate conflict using all five styles, you probably tend to default to one or two. These defaults are influenced by factors such as your view of what conflict is, how you were raised, and your values, beliefs and biases.

Knowing your default style is a helpful starting point, because you can then reflect and analyse how this style might derail you in practice when dealing with conflict situations at work. And then you can start to think about what you might do differently going forward.

For example, if you view conflict as something you either win or lose, your default style is likely competitive. This may mean you don't engage or collaborate with others effectively by listening to their needs because you're more focused on 'winning' the conflict than on finding the right solution. Having this as your default style could end up damaging your relationships in the longer term and see your brand or reputation take a hit inside your organisation. You may also find getting outcomes harder in the long run, as people become less likely to want to work with you. Your relationship currency will decrease. Your performance currency will then also take a hit as it becomes more difficult to achieve outcomes with people.

Conversely, defaulting to a style of conflict avoidance could also have a negative impact on your career currency and your leadership capability. As an example of this, in one of my workshops I asked people where they saw themselves on the Thomas-Kilmann Model. A participant shouted out, 'I don't avoid conflict. When my team doesn't do something the way I need it done, I'll just get it done myself'. Almost as soon as the words came out of his mouth, the lightbulb went off for him. As leaders, being able to be assertive *and* cooperative in the way you lead through conflict conversations is critical.

So, how can you be collaborative in your conflict resolution? A collaborative approach means being open to working with those in the conflict to see how you can find an outcome that meets the needs of both parties *and* still solves the challenge at hand. Your ability to do that well though will always come back to this: **Know yourself and your default styles.**

Understand what kind of conflict you're in

Conflicts in organisations almost always boil down to one (or more) of four things:

1. **The 'What'.** You don't agree on what needs to happen.
2. **The 'How'.** You agree on what needs to happen, but not on how it needs to happen.

3. **The 'Who'.** You don't agree or are unclear on the decision-making criteria, and on who has authority to make decisions.

4. **The 'You'.** You have different working or communication styles that are causing a breakdown of trust.

If you can diagnose what kind of conflict you're in, you will be in a much better position to get to an effective solution quicker. How do you do that? You ask more and talk less.

Ask targeted questions to draw out the challenges your colleagues see. Are they what you see too, or are they different? If you aren't sure where to start with targeted questions, use the QR code at the back of this book and follow the prompts to access my conflict questions cheat sheet.

Avoid global language in conflict

I was once privy to the following conversation in a previous corporate HR role:

Employee: You never recognise me for the work I do. You're always on your phone and never listen to what I am saying.

Team leader: Of course I recognise you, and I'm not always on my phone.

The conversation wasn't going well, obviously.

What I found interesting as I was observing this conversation unfold was that, until this moment, the conversation had been proceeding in a fairly measured and constructive way. However, at the point that global language started being used – with 'never' and 'always' – it all fell apart.

In his decades of work on what makes relationships work, John Gottman speaks to the importance of not using global language – or talking in absolutes – as a key tool in keeping conflicts constructive.

Global language is the use of words and phrases such as 'always', 'never', 'everything', 'all the time', 'everyone' and 'we all'. This kind of language ignites defence in someone and takes away from the topic that the issue is actually about.

That was exactly what happened in the conversation I was privy to. The conversation became less about moving forward with a solution and more about proving or disproving that they each didn't 'always' or 'never' do something. If you want to increase your performance currency in your organisation and get results through and with people, be aware of your use of global language.

Conflict navigation in 3-2-1

As a final point on learning how to navigate conflict well, I recommend reflecting on three core considerations when you need to navigate a conflict conversation.

Firstly, be clear on your real goal. Go into the conversation with clarity on what you actually need from this conversation. *Hint:* it won't be that you need to prove yourself as correct, but it might be that you need consensus on a pathway forward.

Secondly, get clear on what the commonalities are. Yes, you disagree on certain things, which you'll need to diagnose, but it is also important to confirm what you do agree on. For example, a commonality could be that both parties agree success means having a concise and consistent approach across the organisation on how a report is distributed. Great! You've found common ground – now you can work backwards from there.

And lastly, focus on the ways you can demonstrate you are sincerely trying to understand the other party's perspectives, instead of just pushing your own. To move forward with a solution to a conflict in a sustainable way, all parties to the conversation must feel heard. And you show that you're hearing someone by asking questions, playing what you're hearing back to confirm alignment, and empathising.

Maybe you're seeing by now that showing people you are really listening to them is a quintessential superpower for driving a career forward more on happy and less on endless hustling. We're not done yet, however. Now, let's look at improving performance currency via the lens of feedback.

Your Happy Career Action

To start understanding your own default conflict style/s more, ask yourself the following questions:

- How would you define what conflict is? What does it mean to you?
- Finish this sentence: 'I see conflict as an opportunity to...'
- When you observe a conversation becoming tense or getting a little heated, how do you feel? What happens in your body? How do you tend to respond?
- How do you think your colleagues would describe your approach to conflict? What do they see you do and say? How do they see you behave?

Mastering the full menu of feedback – get, give and receive it well

On a scale from one to 'I'd like to gouge my eyes out with a fork', how comfortable are you with feedback conversations? Do you enjoy them, or do you avoid them at all costs – or, if you can't avoid them, count down the minutes until they are over? As with conflict, whether you are comfortable with it or not, feedback is a skill that must be learnt if you want to increase your performance currency and drive a successful career on your terms.

When people talk about feedback, they usually only talk about the process of giving feedback. Don't get me wrong, this is an important skill; however, what is often neglected and overlooked, but is equally as critical, are the skills of asking for feedback *and* receiving feedback well.

Firstly, the quality of the way in which you *ask* for feedback will dictate the quality of feedback you get in return. Asking for feedback allows you to broaden your perspective, gives you insights into your strengths that you might not have even been aware of, and highlights any blind spots that you might want to start focusing your energy into.

Secondly, the way you *receive* feedback – and what you do with it afterwards – will impact your credibility and the perception of your true motivation to grow within the company by those who have given it to you. Receiving feedback well goes a long way to building a strong brand.

Let me delve into each of these processes.

Asking for feedback well

I view asking for feedback well as the omelette of the feedback world – where fewer ingredients make a more delicious meal than just a smash-up of everything on offer. Let me explain.

Have you ever asked for feedback, only to not get any at all? Or, if you do get feedback, it's not specific or helpful enough for you to actually *do* something with? How do you get feedback that you can actually use?

According to professor and organisational psychology specialist Adam Grant, breaking the ice when asking for feedback by giving yourself negative feedback first is key. Grant argues that people often hold back when giving feedback because they are afraid of hurting the other person's feelings. However, when you first acknowledge what you think you're doing wrong, 'the fear melts away'. Grant advises:

Start by saying something like, 'I know that I tend to work quickly and sometimes overlook important details. I'd like to get better at that. What thoughts do you have on how I could improve?' And then, once you have them talking, you could ask, 'And is there anything else I could be working on to improve right now?'

In addition to owning your opportunities first, keep the following in mind when seeking feedback that is helpful for your growth:

- **Ask regularly and in 'real-ish time'.** If you only ask for feedback once or twice a year, it's natural to feel anxious about the process. However, if you integrate feedback conversations into the way you work, it becomes much easier. Be sure to ask in 'real time' too, meaning shortly after an event. For example, if you want feedback on a presentation you just did, ask your stakeholders within a few days, not months later.

- **Widen your lens.** Your manager is highly influential in terms of your promotions, your performance reviews, and potentially the opportunities you do or don't get; however, they are not the only person you can or should seek feedback from. Widen your lens, but be specific and intentional about who you're asking for feedback from. Make sure to approach people who actually engage with you, regularly, people who see your work or are in meetings with you and more importantly, people who may yield some influence in the decisions that are made. (Hello, relationship currency!)

- **Ask skilfully with open questions.** This tip, in my opinion, is far and away the most important, yet it is often the one people spend the least amount of time reflecting on. As mentioned, the way you ask for feedback will dictate the quality of the feedback you get in return. This means focusing on *how* you ask your questions. Generally speaking, the two kinds of questions are open or closed. An open question requires a deeper response than just a yes or no answer. Think about the response you'll likely get to the question 'Do you like summer?' versus 'What is your favourite thing about summer?', for example. These two different questions will elicit two different responses and conversations. Typically, open questions start with 'what', 'how', or 'when', so be purposeful with the way that you ask for feedback using these. This will give you a far greater chance of receiving detailed feedback that's useful and helpful.

Receiving feedback like a pro

In contrast to the omelette, I view receiving feedback as the boiled egg of feedback – in that once it's boiled over and cracked, there's no going back.

How do you think you'd respond to 'Are you open to receiving feedback?'

'Yes, of course' is what most people would say. And this was the response I received when I provided feedback to an employee undergoing a performance improvement plan – right before they threw a stapler at me after receiving said feedback. They'd boiled over.

As you can probably guess, this example doesn't fall into the category of receiving feedback well.

Here's another, less extreme, version you may relate to. I had provided feedback to a team member of my own. Before I had finished sharing my feedback, they had already clenched their jaw, crossed their arms and begun cutting me off demanding examples (which I was about to provide).

This type of response may resonate more with you. Hell, perhaps you've even done something similar yourself. (We've all been there.) However, the way you receive feedback, irrespective of how you feel about it, will significantly impact your brand and reputation inside an organisation. Unfortunately, we often don't talk enough about how to receive feedback – so I'm here to fill this gap.

Here are my top three tips for receiving feedback well:

1. **Demonstrate gratitude by saying thank you sincerely.** The sharer of the feedback has taken an emotional risk by being candid and honest in an effort to support you, so let them know you appreciate this effort. How you feel about the feedback at this point is irrelevant.

2. **Listen to the feedback without judgement.** If you respect someone enough to ask them for feedback, or you've said that you are open to receiving it, then listen to it. Give your full attention and resist the urge to cut them off or evaluate the accuracy of things. When you're receiving feedback, it can be easy to tune out from the conversation and transport yourself back to the time the person giving the feedback is referring to and analyse the moment. Try to avoid doing that, and instead be present.

3. **Clarify if you need to, but do not debate or get defensive.** Absolutely ask questions in order to understand more about the feedback or bring it to life for yourself, especially if you can't recall the example being referred to. However, be aware of your tone and whether you are coming from a place of curiosity, as opposed to criticism of the feedback.

These three aspects combine to create the fundamental difference between receiving feedback like a pro and receiving it poorly – or throwing a stapler at someone.

What's also underlying this approach is showing that you want to act on most of the feedback you receive from stakeholders, because firstly, you respect their opinions enough to ask for it, and secondly, you want to demonstrate your interest in growth – both of which increase relationship and performance currency.

When it comes to receiving feedback, though, here is what almost always happens:

- Person A receives feedback from person B.
- Person B leaves the conversation assuming that person A will act on said feedback.
- Person A thanks person B for the feedback and does nothing with it, or does something with it but doesn't tell anyone, especially person B, about it.

Remember to close the loop.

Closing the loop and communicating your actions following the feedback is just as critical as receiving it well in the first place. Doing so ensures your stakeholders know you're taking their feedback seriously. This goes a long way to increasing your credibility and trust inside an organisation, thereby increasing your opportunities over time.

Giving feedback

Finally, giving feedback is the poached egg of feedback – it's either executed well with the perfect amount of goop, or it's a total shemozzle and you end up with a hard egg that just leaves you feeling disappointed.

Let me give you an example of the shemozzle.

It had just gone 9.30 am and I'd already had two conversations with coaching clients about feedback they'd received from their manager that was vague, unspecific and missing examples to provide context.

One coaching client mentioned that their manager even said to them, 'I love how I can give you feedback with ease'. To that manager, the employee seemed to receive the feedback well; however, they had no real idea what the feedback meant and didn't feel comfortable enough to ask.

Broad, sweeping feedback statements such as 'don't overthink', 'take more risks', 'challenge me more' or 'be less pedantic' without any examples to provide detail is lazy leadership at best. Maybe you've been on the receiving end of something like this before and you agree? The result is often a confused – and concerned – employee who is likely going to feel less empowered to make decisions or take action.

I won't sit here and pretend that feedback conversations aren't uncomfortable. They are. But what is interesting is that when they are, it's usually due more to us and the pressure we're putting on ourselves, or the assumptions we are making about how the other party will respond.

Numerous feedback models are available that provide frameworks to map conversations to. When preparing for feedback conversations, I use what I call the SAIF Model (an expansion of the well-known SBI model, coined by the Centre for Creative Leadership). This helps ensure my feedback is specific while still retaining the human element.

The elements in the SAIF Model are situation, action, impact and forward, and table 4 overleaf runs through how these elements come together.

Table 4: The SAIF Model for giving feedback

SAIF Model	What does it mean?	Example
Situation	When did it happen? Who was there? Be clear, and ensure you paint a picture so that your colleague knows exactly what you are referring to.	'Hey Simon, when we were in the meeting last week finalising our annual marketing plan...'
Action	Explain what the behaviour was that you did or didn't like. Be clear here in terms of what was actually said, written, done or not done so that the person has clarity on what happened.	'You came in 20 minutes late and started talking about ideas you had that were not at all relevant to what we were there to discuss, which was to finalise our FY25 strategy, and it really derailed the meeting.'
Impact	Explain the impact of the behaviour specific to you. This is your feedback; therefore, it is your impact. You are not speaking on behalf of others (unless this has been agreed to by others, but I generally advise against this). You are speaking on behalf of yourself, so use 'I' statements, not 'we' statements.	'We needed to make some big decisions in that meeting, and you being late and then distracting the conversation meant I had to stay back and get this done after hours given the deadline. It also meant I missed my kid's basketball game, which I feel disappointed about.'

SAIF Model	What does it mean?	Example
Forward	This is often the missed part in feedback conversations, particularly peer-to-peer ones. Hanging onto negativity after a conversation is helpful to no-one and will only further impact your relationship. After you've said your piece, restate the importance of your working relationship and put something in place for you and your peer to connect on or work on again to ensure the relationship remains positive. Having a challenging conversation like this and then not speaking to your peer again for a few weeks can make it even more awkward than before. Rip off the bandaid and find a way to stay visible to each other.	'I value our working relationship and your input on things immensely, so going forward, I'd appreciate you being on time, but more importantly, helping me ensure we use the limited time we do have to make the decisions we need to. Let's catch up next week to talk about those other ideas you mentioned, though. What do you think?'

Feedback conversations can feel awkward, and at times you might wish the world would just swallow you whole. This is because you're outside your comfort zone.

When you reach outside of your comfort zone, however, you grow. It is also how you exhibit the kinds of leadership behaviours that your workplace needs to see from you, particularly if you want to increase your performance currency and, therefore, increase your career opportunities.

Getting comfortable with the three types of feedback is a critical skill that you need to learn. Start now, and flex those feedback muscles.

Over to you. How are you at asking for, receiving and giving feedback?

Your Happy Career Action

- What is something you are curious to receive some feedback on about yourself? Write down some examples of specific (and open) questions you could ask someone to increase your chances of getting useful feedback. Then, go and have that convo. Remember to own your opportunity for growth first and then ask for the feedback.

- Reflect on a piece of feedback you've received recently and how you've closed the loop on it. Did you report back to the person who gave you the feedback with an update on what you've been trying, testing and noticing? If not, there is no time like the present!

- What is something you have been meaning to give someone feedback about but haven't? (Make sure this relates to something recent.) Practise mapping out this feedback against the SAIF Model, and then see if you can engage in that feedback convo. Remember: this tool can be used for positive and constructive feedback!

Using strategic self-promotion

Picture this: it was a Tuesday morning, 8 am. My coffee hadn't fully seeped into my bloodstream yet, and I already had someone at my desk waiting to speak with me. They clearly were not happy.

'I'm angry that I wasn't given the role' was the first thing to come out of this person's mouth. No 'Good morning. How are you?' Nothing – just this.

'Which role are you talking about?' was my response. I knew what this person currently did, and we had no roles currently being advertised that were an obvious next step for them.

'The marketing manager role', they said. 'I'm angry that Joe didn't offer it to me.'

'I wasn't aware that this was a path you were interested in', I said to this person. I followed this up with, 'How long have you been interested in this space, and who knows about it?'

'Well, no-one technically knows, but that's not the point. I should have been offered the role.' If I'm being 100 per cent honest with you, at this point in my head I absolutely had 'WTF' vibes going on.

What, no steak on a vegetarian menu?

What I've just described was the equivalent of me sitting at a vegetarian restaurant and then being angry at the staff that no-one thought to offer me a steak.

I often speak to people who are upset or disgruntled by the fact that they haven't been offered – handed, even – a particular opportunity. Yet, when I ask them if they have mentioned their interest in the opportunity to their manager or colleague, the answer is often a resounding *no*. Sometimes we can expect others to read our minds and our unique ambitions, aspirations or areas that we *might* want to get involved in that are outside the norm. When we do this, however, we've fallen into the category of the 'hoper'. (If you need a refresher on this quadrant of the Happy Career Matrix, refer to chapter 1.)

This is what then tends to happen. The person who feels they were passed over or ignored for an opportunity becomes more and more resentful, unhappy or disgruntled – at this point still not having said anything about their interest but expecting their manager or colleagues to know. Am I suggesting that managers don't own some responsibility for understanding and appreciating the unique aspirations and development goals of their people? Absolutely not. But, peeps – this isn't enough. Leaving your goals and dreams in the hands of others is not the answer. All it gives you is someone to blame when those dreams don't come true and a reason to become unhappy or resentful.

If you want to increase your performance currency, you must consistently and gracefully put your enthusiasm for learning and growth out there. You must demonstrate the proactive steps that you are taking to develop yourself, too. And you must operate from the 'happy' quadrant, not the 'hoper' quadrant. So, how do you do this in a way that feels smooth and controlled, without making it all about you?

Share the stage to self-promote

Recently, I had a session with a wonderful client of mine. As part of our work, she reached out to some key leaders in her working world to learn more about their careers and role priorities, increase her business acumen and understand more about what they specifically look for in leaders. (In other words, she was building her relationship currency.)

What my client did so well here was that she shared the stage to self-promote. She took a genuine interest in learning from other leaders to build her own knowledge base, while also inserting into the conversation her career aspirations and the actions she had taken to develop herself.

This client later fed back to me that, when chatting to these leaders about her interest in a future leadership role, one of the leaders said, 'Ohhh, I'd never even considered you for a role in this space. I had no idea that was something you were interested in. I'm so glad you mentioned it!'

That is why it is so important that you make your ambitions known. In my client's case, she is now on the radar when it comes to leadership opportunities, and has even locked in a secondment opportunity to stretch herself and her leadership skills.

It is essential that you have conversations with people about where you want to go and what you want to achieve in your career. Or, if you don't know where you want to go, it is just as important that you have those conversations too, and start to look at ways in which you can 'expand to land' by learning other parts of the business to find out what might light you up.

Remember: wanting and getting aren't always the same thing.

Am I saying that by making your goals and aspirations known the next time an opportunity comes around, it will be yours on a platter? No, I am not. But putting yourself out there puts you in great stead for that opportunity, or at least will get you feedback and development advice on what you need to do to attain that opportunity in the future.

Continuing to close the loop with stakeholders who have taken the time to talk to you about your career aspirations, and telling them the proactive steps you're taking to upskill yourself, will also keep you on the radar as someone motivated and enthusiastic – which is important for increasing your performance currency.

Over to you. What are your goals, and how can you strategically self-promote?

Your Happy Career Action

Now is a great time to go back to the first element of the five-part career framework (chapter 3) and revisit your career values and definition of success. Reflect on those, and write out your aspirations and some short- and medium-term goals for yourself. Where would you like to be in 12 months' time? What areas of the business are you curious to learn more about? What skills do you need to focus on to get you there? Outlining three to five SMART (specific, measurable, achievable, relevant and time-bound) goals is a great target to set yourself.

Once you've captured these goals, ask yourself who knows about your aspirations. What conversations, if any, have you had with your manager about the things that interest you? If you aren't sure what your next career step might be, that's okay too. Who can you reach out to at your organisation or externally to understand more about the kinds of roles that are out there? Conversations, as always, are key.

Challenge yourself to have one conversation a month in which you talk about your aspirations, learn more about growth opportunities, or talk about the learnings you're also having by developing yourself.

As you can see, building a strong performance currency is about more than just knowing a lot of 'stuff'. Technical expertise is important, but expertise alone isn't what enables you to solve problems, collaborate effectively or ensure your stakeholders see what you are capable of. Strong performance currency is built by taking what you know and getting results that drive an organisation forward – targeting your effort, expertise *and* enthusiasm to get outcomes. This is what sees your career move from hustle to happy.

Key takeaways

Here's the fourth element in a nutshell:

- To increase your performance currency, you must know the business that you're in and how your role contributes to the organisation's success.

- Communication is key to getting outcomes at work. People are overwhelmed by the information competing for their limited attention every day. Make sure you're giving them a reason to pay attention to you.

- Managing conflict effectively is a critical skill for getting results from your hard work. You've got to be able to navigate conflict well in order to keep your currency high.

- Getting, giving and receiving feedback like a pro shows your capacity for growth and opportunities. How you ask for feedback, the way in which you receive it and your ability to deliver it well all tie into your performance currency.

- Be consistent and strategic about self-promotion to ensure that your stakeholders know who you are, what you're capable of, where you want to go, and what you are doing to help get yourself there.

Chapter 7

Element Five: Future-proofing yourself!

Up until this point, all elements of my five-part career framework have been giving you tools and considerations to set yourself up for success, with a focus on now. But what about ensuring you are remaining happy and relevant into the future? This final element looks at the skills and attitudes you need to ensure you stay relevant in a world that isn't slowing down. I look at how to get beyond the ladder in your career, and why it is so important that you continue to look up and around you when it comes to staying ahead of the career game. Lastly, at some point in your career (if not already!) you'll need to negotiate for something that you want, so I teach you how to do so in a way that ensures you put your best foot forward.

But first, let's talk about how resilience and roller-coasters are relevant to a career built more on happy and less on hustle!

Resilience – learning to love the theme park!

In 2012, I visited the United Arab Emirates (UAE) with my husband. As part of his birthday present, I took him to Ferrari World in

Abu Dhabi. At that time, and still at the time of writing, Ferrari World has the fastest roller-coaster in the world – taking you from 0 to 250 kilometres an hour in 3 seconds. We got the VIP park pass so that we didn't have to wait in lines and could go on the roller-coaster over and over again.

Because this roller-coaster was *so* hardcore, they make you wear special goggles to go on it and leave behind any garments that could blow off. Given it was about 48 degrees Celsius outside in Abu Dhabi, and we were in a designated tourist zone, I was just wearing a black dress with singlet-style straps.

We got onto the roller-coaster cart with four others. We were in the front seat of the ride with our goggles on. Just before we took off, I had a feeling I'd probably not put my goggles on tightly enough, but it was too late to check now. The safety bar was down. We were locked in and the green light had just gone off.

Zooooooooosh. I was right. My goggles weren't on properly. Within two seconds of taking off, the g-force had thrown them right off my head and into the abyss. With the fear of death in me about the power of this ride, I squeezed my eyes closed for the whole thing, too scared to open them in case my eye balls literally got torn out of my head, or something flew into them and blinded me for life.

As we continued on the ride, my eyes squeezed completely shut, I also started to feel an excessive breeze around my chest area. There was definitely something exposed, and a general feeling of something *flapping* around.

I signalled to my husband to look because I couldn't open my eyes. *'Claire!!!!!!'* He burst out in total horror, while also grabbing the side of my shoulder and my dress, trying to put me back together. The top half of my dress had completely blown open and exposed me – right in the time for the standard roller-coaster ride picture.

Flash.

Eventually, the ride came to an abrupt end back where we started, and I hurriedly fixed my clothes. I felt mortified, having flashed everyone in one of the most conservative places on earth.

We headed out from the ride and past the photo zone. There I was in all my glory on the big screen for all to see. I ran over, panicked, and begged them to take the photo down. Once they realised why, they quickly deleted it in horror and shook their heads at me.

At this point, you could assume we were done with this particular ride. No, not my husband. He wanted to go straight back on again so that I could fully see it and enjoy it. So, we headed back down, and I tightened my dress within an inch of its life – so tight I almost couldn't breathe. It was definitely not going anywhere this time. I grabbed my safety goggles and secured them on my head tightly enough that little rolls of eye fat were spilling out around the edges. They weren't going anywhere, either. We got into the front row, ready to take it all in again.

ZOOOOOOOOOSH. We took off. I forgot to take a breath before the green light went, and this time the g-force hit me so hard in the chest that I fainted.

The ride continued to fling itself around the course, with me flopping around like a lifeless bobble head. When I finally came to, my eyes opened to an almighty flash. There it was again, that dreaded picture. (See appendix for a copy. *Kidding!* Made you look, though.)

'How epic was that?' said my husband as we came to a stop.

I had no idea how 'epic' it was because I'd flopped about through the whole thing, feeling largely out of control for most of it with little memory of how I'd gotten to where I was.

Your career is like a roller-coaster

Just as with roller-coasters, your career will have highs, and it will have lows. You will experience incredible parts you never want to end. And then you will have parts in the journey when you feel out of control, exposed and vulnerable, and you just want a project, period or experience to be over already. These hard times require you to be resilient.

In order to strengthen my own career resilience, I like to remember this analogy of careers having stages similar to those of a roller-coaster. You have the high points, the flat points and the low points. And you also have the plunge-you-upside-down-outside-of-your-own-body-feeling-like-you're-so-not-prepared-forthis points.

In my career, I've experienced every part of the roller-coaster. And I'm sure the same will be true for you – if it isn't already. When it comes to acknowledging these stages of the ride, though, and then best supporting yourself through them, I've noticed that as humans we have some bad habits.

When we're in a good place – aka the slow and steady rise to the top as the ride starts – we can spend all of our time trying to make it great, anticipating and wanting to rush to what is next. When we are in a great place, we're either too 'busy' to realise it and be truly present in it, *or* we're so terrified of when it's going to end that we don't allow ourselves to enjoy it. Yet, when we are in a bad or a terrible place, we feel like it has gone on forever, with no signs of the end in sight. This place is deep, and it's heavy. And it often feels exhausting. We can feel as if are stuck in the hustle and we just can't get out.

Over the course of my career, I have had major promotions and incredible travel opportunities, and worked with brilliant teams. I've also been made redundant, dealt with some of the most horrific HR issues that you can imagine, had multiple setbacks and disappointments, and often had to deal with these while also navigating personal challenges.

Here are three things I know to be true based on all these experiences:

1. **Sometimes you have to zoom out and look at the whole ride.**
   Get some perspective over all parts of the ride. When you're in a super scary part of the ride, it won't last forever. It *will* pass. And you *will* rise again. Equally, the good and great climbs and turns don't last forever, so enjoy them. Embrace them. Be present in them, and be grateful for them. When you step back and zoom out a little, you are more able to gain perspective about yourself and your career overall. You are able to see the low parts of the ride for what they are – just part of the experience, *not* the whole experience.

2. **You have to sit in the front seat for the full experience.**
   To truly get the most out of your career, you've got to be in the front seat of the roller-coaster. Does this mean vulnerability and risk? Absolutely. Does this mean your goggles might fly off and you'll be completely blind to what might be coming? Heck yes. Can you experience only the good from the front seat, and shelter yourself from the bad? Absolutely not. But will you look back at your career knowing you gave it everything you had and didn't just sit at the back being a 'hoper', waiting for something to happen for you? Hell yes!

3. **People will be on different rides at different times to you.**
   Stop comparing – otherwise, you'll rob yourself of any and all joy. You may have friends who had a steep and quick ascension to their definition of success really early on in their career, but then they may plateau and do a total career flip years later. You may have taken longer to find a career that lights you up, but now you're there you see how all your previous experiences were necessary to give you the clarity you have now. Run your own race, in your own lane, in your own time.

At this point, you might be wondering how my roller-coaster story ends. Did I try again? Did I sit in the front seat? Did I acknowledge that this too shall pass?

The answer is yes. We got back on. Goggles in place? Check. Dress on tightly? Check. A deep breath taken before take-off? Check.

Let's do this! And we did.

Building resilience and agility – and antifragility

In *Emotional Agility*, renowned management strategist (and co-founder of the Harvard/McLean Institute of Coaching) Susan David talks about the idea of emotional agility, arguing it is a necessary tool to help you navigate and understand your own thoughts and feelings, particularly in the complex and fast-changing knowledge landscape we all live in. This management of your own thoughts and feelings, she says, is 'essential to business success'. According to David:

> *Effective leaders don't buy into or try to suppress their inner experiences. Instead, they approach them in a mindful, values-driven, and productive way – developing what we call emotional agility.*

David highlights that improving your emotional agility can help you 'alleviate stress, reduce errors, become more innovative, and improve job performance'.

You no doubt know by now that resilience is critical in your career if you are to deal with setbacks and challenges, particularly if you are playing the long game (which you should be!). And you need to build your emotional agility to help you process those feelings and emotions with awareness, understanding and greater flexibility so you can navigate the setbacks.

But what about your ability to also be a little more gritty in the process? Controversial, maybe, but is there a place for you to be a little less fragile? Nassim Nicholas Taleb thinks so, and he talks about this in his book *Antifragile: Things that gain from disorder*.

As Taleb highlights, 'Antifragility is beyond resilience or robustness. The resilient resists shocks and stays the same; the antifragile gets better'. When building careers more on happy and less on hustle, can you find a way to not only move through the setbacks with resilience, but also come out the other side stronger and even better for having had them?

I think you have to, especially if you acknowledge the pace at which your working world and skill requirements are changing.

Getting beyond the ladder

Did you know that on average, working people will likely have between five and seven careers across their working lives? Not five to seven jobs – five to seven different career paths. Meaning if you are currently a lawyer but you have a deep yearning to be a belly dancer, it is so *not* off the cards for you. But a career change does require a very significant commitment from you – involving curiosity, agility and lifelong learning.

You'll remember I touched on Carol Dweck's book *Mindset* back in chapter 3 in relation to the first element of my five-part career framework. In *Mindset*, Dweck references Benjamin Barber, a prominent political theorist, who stated, 'I don't divide the world into the weak and the strong, or the successes and the failures... I divide the world into the learners and the non-learners'.

In our current world, at the rate at which it is evolving, I couldn't agree more. We're living longer and working longer, but in jobs and industries that are changing quicker than we can keep up with. What does this mean for us? The great news is that employers are placing greater value on individuals who are agile, flexible and able to learn and adapt well to change. Transferable skills – such as self-awareness, resilience, curiosity, lifelong learning, social awareness, empathy and technological aptitude – are all becoming increasingly more valuable, and in some ways more so than technical skills.

Embracing the non-linear career path

The one-directional, rigid and narrow career ladder is out, and the non-linear career is in. And this is an exciting place to be to future-proof yourself, *if* you can keep the discipline to continue to learn.

What actually makes someone choose to be a non-learner, though? After all, we're all born with almost an automatic drive to learn, aren't we? Consider how new babies learn to walk and talk, eat, read signals, and everything in between. These are not insignificant learning opportunities – rather, these are some of the most difficult tasks to learn in our lifetimes. And yet, as babies, we do them without question.

Dweck gets clear about what it really is that puts an end to our openness to learning. Yep, we're back at the power of mindset again. Through her study of thousands of people from preschoolers on, Dweck is able to highlight the different approaches of those with a fixed mindset versus those with a growth mindset. Dweck says:

As soon as children become able to evaluate themselves, some of them become afraid of challenges. They become afraid of not being smart… it's breathtaking how many reject an opportunity to learn.

Dweck outlines working with four year olds and offering them a choice – to redo a puzzle they had already solved, or try a harder one. The children with more of a fixed mindset, who wanted to make sure they succeeded and didn't make a mistake, chose to redo the easy puzzle. The children with more of a growth mindset, however, who believed they could stretch themselves and get smarter, chose the harder puzzle.

Wanting to do the easy puzzle is one thing, but wanting to take the 'easy' opportunity in your career is a whole other decision to make – and it has a considerable impact on your happiness and fulfilment in the longer term.

Finding time for learning

In the movie *In Time*, Justin Timberlake stars as factory worker Will Salas, operating in a dystopian world where the primary currency to survive is time. The rich have it by the truckload, while the poor and working class hustle harder and harder to get more of it. Although the premise of this movie is that you actually need to have time on your 'clock' to survive, the idea of wanting more and more time feels equally relevant to the world we live in today.

We all say, 'I wish I had more time', or 'I just need more hours in the day to get my work done'. But my question is this: to do what specifically with it? To continue to pedal harder and squeeze even more things into your day? What if instead of just wishing you had more time, you just made better use of the time you have?

I believe you have only two real ways to do this effectively: boundaries and discipline.

I recall a time I received an email from my then-CEO. After reading an article he liked the look of, he had forwarded it on to me after hours with the comment, 'This is cool. I'd like to look at this too'.

I'd made the decision to read my emails at night, saw this one from him, and thought, *OMG, how I am going to pull something together for our conversation tomorrow*. I ended up staying up until midnight putting my thoughts together and getting ready to respond ahead of our catch-up the next day.

When we caught up, I brought the article up and his response was, 'Oh, yeah, that was in no way urgent. It was just a thought I had that I wanted to share with you'.

I had done two significant things here that were not enabling me to hold a boundary and live a career built on happy and not on hustle.

Firstly, I wasn't holding any kind of boundary. A boundary of mine should have been that I stop checking my emails after a certain time at night so I could focus on other parts of my life that were important, giving me the fuel to stay energised and enthusiastic.

Secondly, I hadn't gone back to my CEO with any clarifying questions to understand more about what he was hoping to discuss, how important or urgent it was, and what outcome he was actually hoping for. Instead, I panicked and made assumptions, and then filled the gaps with my own meaning. And my overall assumption was that in order to prove myself as the 'best worker', I had to reply now and do this now (which in *no* way was ever an expectation that he had of me).

I want to make two clear points here:

1. **Boundaries aren't just about saying no.** If you're struggling to hold boundaries at work, it may be because you associate boundaries with just saying no to something and worry you're going to come across as difficult or unhelpful. The hustle issue then comes into play when you mindlessly say yes to everything, or act without clarifying needs or requirements or understanding what success looks like. You can be useful in many ways, have a strong positive impact *and* still hold a personal boundary.

2. **Discipline is the key.** What might also be getting in the way is not so much your ability to hold a boundary but your discipline to do so. You likely then get frustrated because you don't have enough time to do it all. You can only prioritise so many things. And don't think more time-management hacks will be

the solution to your problems. Nope. What is needed is the discipline to take a step back regularly to think about what the true priorities are, and what the most meaningful contribution is that you can make with the time you have.

Entrepreneur Steven Bartlett, author of *Diary of a CEO* (and host of the podcast of the same name), is a global sensation for a number of reasons, often speaking to sold-out crowds all over the globe. In his recent book he had this to say about the idea of time management and discipline:

> *There is no time-management system, procrastination-ending method or productivity hack that's going to give you the under-lying thing you need in order to stay the course, make the right decisions and focus on what matters over the long term – discipline.*

As Bartlett highlights, without your own internal discipline, none of the 'hundreds of available methods, hacks and tricks' will work. So, if you want to future-proof yourself for the long term and enjoy a sustainable, happy career, be disciplined with your boundaries and regularly review your priorities.

Ensuring you stay relevant in a world that isn't slowing down

Needing to stay relevant and almost constantly reinvent yourself may feel like a fairly new pressure, but the truth is this has always been our reality – it's just become even more prevalent given the pace we operate at now.

What is exciting about this concept is that it is a choice, and it's entirely within your control as to if and how you stay relevant. The movie *Hidden Figures* provides a perfect example of this.

We're all really just a bunch of NASA computers

Hidden Figures is based on the true story of three women who made important contributions to America's NASA space programs both before and after the 'human computers' were replaced by digital computers. Octavia Spencer plays the role of Dorothy Vaughan, who supervises the 'coloured computers'.

Dorothy sees that digital computers are the way of the future and makes the decision to teach herself the prototype programming language FORTRAN (now Fortran) in order to keep herself relevant and ahead of the change curve.

In a pivotal scene in the movie, two male engineers had been trying to navigate the room-sized IBM computer without success. They'd spent hours trying to figure out what it was, how it worked, and how to get it going. Dorothy, seeing the opportunity and having invested time into learning the program, walked into the room (after hours), pulled the plug out from one place and plugged it into another, and the machine immediately started. Later, the same men find her processing code, and they look at her completely shocked as to how she knew what to do.

From there, Dorothy advocated for her team to also learn the new programming language so that they could all remain valuable and relevant to NASA.

Dorothy had a choice here. She could sit back and wait for the digital computer to take her and her team's jobs, or she could get out in front of it. She chose the second option – choosing to be curious, growth-minded and a learner, instead of redundant, stale and eventually forced to change, or forced out completely.

Refuse to become irrelevant

I have had many conversations over my career that will never leave me. One of those was part of having to stand down an entire workforce because it was no longer a commercially viable part of the business. Employees were given over a year's notice that the workplace was closing down, as well as ample transition support and considerable severance options.

In particular, what has always stayed with me is the choice made by those who successfully transitioned, and by those who didn't. Those who successfully transitioned did so because they chose to make themselves relevant. They looked at what was changing in their world and made sure they upskilled themselves in the areas they needed to within the time frames that they had. They didn't put their heads in the sand and avoid it. Those who didn't successfully transition found themselves irrelevant in a world that had moved on from them. Harsh? Yes. True? Also yes. The world isn't slowing down for anyone. It is up to you to remain vigilant to the things that are changing in your career and ensure that you adapt accordingly.

The World Economic Forum's *Future of Jobs Report 2023* states that two-fifths of the core skills workers have today will be disrupted by technological change by 2027. This means that half of all workers' core skills will need to be updated every five years. It's no surprise, then, that curiosity and lifelong learning are among the top ten human skills you need to succeed.

But here's the thing – when you are in a constant state of hustle, moving from meeting to meeting and task to task, you aren't looking up and around. You go to work every day. You work through your task list, achieving what's being asked. And you work pretty darn hard.

These things are important to your performance and, ultimately, to ensuring you are getting the job done; however, when you are too focused on the day-to-day tasks, you can find yourself looking up and around one day and realising that the world has shifted. Your industry has changed.

If you're not looking up and out, you aren't seeing the forest from the trees. You are just surviving. And in this state, you can wake up one day and realise almost all the trees have been chopped down. The forest is gone. Just the one tree you've been using for shade for so long remains. I don't want this for you.

How do you stay relevant in your job, industry and organisation? To help future-proof yourself, you can complete a SWOT analysis twice a year as part of your personal career strategy. A strategic tool generally used in business, in this case you can use the SWOT analysis to audit your strengths (S), weaknesses (W), opportunities (O) and threats (T) against internal and external conditions. You then use your responses to reflect on yourself, your career pathway and the industry you're currently in.

Not sure where to start? Jump to the QR code at the back of the book and follow the prompts to access my personal career SWOT template. And you can also do some research and your own reflection using the questions in the following action box.

Over to you.

Your Happy Career Action

Take some time to work through the following questions specific to your career pathway and/or the industry you are in.

- Is your industry or career pathway generally growing, or is it contracting? What are some of the reasons behind this?
- How are technological advancements reshaping the skills required in your industry or career pathway?
- How is the increasing focus on sustainability influencing practices within your industry or career?

- In what ways are automation and artificial intelligence affecting job roles and responsibilities in your role and/or industry?
- What new regulations or policies are on the horizon that could significantly impact you?
- What emerging trends or disruptive technologies do you foresee having the greatest impact on your industry or career in the next decade?
- Based on your responses to the preceding questions, what are some of the key skills you need to focus on developing to remain relevant?

Staying proactive and curious about the changes happening around you doesn't need to be scary or boring. When you choose to develop skills such as curiosity and lifelong learning, the changes in your career or industry can become fun, and you can ensure you continue to target your growth efforts, develop your expertise and channel your enthusiasm into ensuring you are set up for a future that makes you happy.

Negotiating your value and getting what you want at work

Inevitably in your career a time will come, if it hasn't already, when you'll need to negotiate for yourself. Being able to do this effectively is an essential part of future-proofing yourself and putting yourself in the best position to enjoy a career that lights you up and is built on happy rather than hustle. But there is an art to this – actually, an art and a science.

Over the years, I have been witness to, or have been on the receiving end of, hundreds of requests for pay rises, promotions, training opportunities, secondments and much, much more. Interestingly, the requests that were approved had a few things in common. I've boiled down those commonalities and can now give you my top tips for getting what you want at work.

Start with the end in mind

Before you approach your manager, spend some time figuring out exactly what it is that you want and why you want it. That might sound obvious, but just saying 'I want more money because I deserve it' isn't really enough. Consider why you feel you are deserving, and how important it is to you.

If you do get what you're asking for, think about how that will affect you – will it inspire and further motivate you to improve your skills? And what about if you don't get it – could you still show up as a key contributor, or will you want to look elsewhere? Start with the end in mind, and be really clear on what it is you're asking for and why it matters to you.

Do the work

Preparation is key here. If you really want to put your best foot forward and get what you want, put the time in up-front to maximise your chances of getting it. You need to assess your current performance and get honest with yourself. For instance, don't just go up to your boss or manager and immediately ask for a raise without any justification behind it. Do some market research first, making sure you're comparing apples with apples. Look for similar roles in similar-sized businesses in the industry you're in. Is your salary in line with the standard for others? If not, you may be able to use it as justification for a pay request.

Capture any key accomplishments, achievements and deliverables over the last 6 to 12 months and include those as part of your request. If you have over-delivered in any areas, now is the time to put that to work. Speak the language of the business, and talk in outcomes, not inputs (revisit chapter 6 if needed).

Communicate your message properly

Now that you know why your request is important to you, and you've done some preparation and research, think about what would be important to your boss in this conversation. What would they be considering? Prepare to talk to those points up-front. As much as you may want a pay rise because you believe you deserve it, it probably isn't the way your manager needs to hear it. Again, jump back to the communication tips in chapter 6 if needed. Why should your manager grant your request?

Consider potential barriers to your request

Get ahead of any resistance by thinking ahead and anticipating any existing barriers that could hinder you from getting what you want at work. For example, say you're asking to reduce to a four-day work week, but you still want to be paid at a full-time salary. The kinds of questions you could anticipate from your manager could include, 'How will you manage certain meetings that might land on the day you want to have off?' or, 'How will you manage responses to your customers, or your team?' Talking to these before being asked demonstrates your proactivity at ensuring a solution that works for everyone.

Put pen to paper on what your request actually is – and submit it to your manager

Personally, I'm a big fan of getting your thoughts together, putting them in writing and sending that to your manager ahead of time. Firstly, this ensures you're able to put your best foot forward and communicate in the way that you want to from the get-go. Secondly, you're not blindsiding your manager. You're sending them the information with all of your research ahead of time, and then saying to them, 'I wanted to give you time to read through my request and digest it. Then we can sit down and expand on that further in a conversation next week'. They're likely going to feel you have respected them enough to give them time to absorb your request, and then prepare for that conversation as well.

Be present during the conversation (and practise ahead of time!)

Practise, practise, practise how you want to present yourself in that conversation. On the day of the meeting, take a few moments to ensure you're in a positive mindset. Get to the room (or the call) early if you can so that you 'own' the space. During the conversation, make it clear you are listening to what your manager is saying, and don't be so preoccupied with your own thoughts or worries that you fail to be truly present.

Don't react poorly if you don't get the outcome you want

If you go back to the section in chapter 6 on the importance of receiving feedback well, you'll know why your reactions matter. If you don't get what you want in this conversation, throwing a tantrum will absolutely ensure you won't get it, or much else, going forward. Stay calm, stay cool, and instead ask questions from a place of curiosity and a desire to understand. Aim to leave the conversation open for a follow-up, or revisit in another few months based on an agreed set of actions happening.

Being able to negotiate for yourself is a key part of future-proofing yourself, your growth and your value inside the organisation. Make it count.

Key takeaways

Here's the fifth element in a nutshell:

- The world will keep throwing you curveballs, so resilience, emotional agility and antifragility are all skills you need in order to thrive in the future of work.

- Staying relevant in your career means remaining curious and being a lifelong learner. Both of these are active choices that you can make.

- Careers are no longer built on the ladder, and this is a good thing. Your transferable skills are highly valuable, and opportunities are endless if you create them for yourself.

- Boundaries and discipline are key to making space for learning and growth, both of which can get lost when you get stuck wearing your 'busyness' badge.

- You will need to negotiate for yourself in your career, and doing so well is an art and science. Preparation is key.

Conclusion

Time to build your career game plan

Well, my friend, there you have it – you've just learnt my five-part career framework to help you enjoy a long-term career built more on happy and less on hustle.

By now I hope that you see this book was never about telling you not to have a strong work ethic; instead, it is about teaching you how to take that strong work ethic and target it to get better outcomes from your effort, expertise and enthusiasm.

This book was written for you to disrupt the cycle of 'busyness', hustle and hope as a career success strategy, and instead empower yourself with real-world tools to create a strategy that excites you. Why? Because those who are fulfilled and can find meaning in their work and their impact are naturally better performers and more satisfied humans.

And when employees perform better and are more satisfied, organisations win. The world wins.

Now, it's up to you.

Think back all the way to chapter 1 and my Happy Career Matrix (HCM). Ask yourself – will you live in the space of the hustler, the hoper or the haphazard, *or* will you embrace a happy career and life?

Where to from here?

I have some further help available for individuals, and for teams and organisations.

Individuals

The learning never ends. If you want access to some of the bonus extras and templates I reference throughout the book, use the QR code below and follow the prompts. You'll continue to learn and grow your happy career.

Teams and organisations

This book is just the start. If you have found it insightful and helpful, and are interested in taking these learnings to your team or your organisation, I would love to continue a conversation with you.

Together, we can create an army of employees capable of targeting their effort, expertise and enthusiasm in ways that get results for your company now and into the future.

I work with organisations globally in person, online and onstage, and it would be my pleasure to support you or your team at your next conference, training day, staff retreat or anything in between. Reach out to me at claire@claireseeber.com.au or visit my website at www.claireseeber.com.au. I look forward to connecting with you.

About the author

Claire Seeber believes that the world needs more heart and more humour – and a greater ability to have real and honest conversations, human to human. Claire has spent more than 16 years helping individuals to *be* the best talent and organisations to *keep* their best talent.

She is an expert in leadership development and career advancement, and blends her experience in business, human resources and communications to ensure that people are better able to show up and have the impact on themselves, their teams and their organisations that they can feel proud of *and* that get results.

As a career and leadership coach, trainer and speaker, Claire has worked with or for some of the world's most well-known brands, including Fortescue Metals Group, Chevron, Superdry, Mineral Resources, Colgate-Palmolive and NBC Universal.

Claire is an IECL-accredited coach and is Human Synergistics and DISC accredited. She is the founder of Eating your Cake too and co-founder of the Future Female Leaders Program, with both organisations supporting her personal mission of closing the gender leadership gap in her lifetime.

References

References listed in order of mention.

Preface

Dattani, S, Rodés-Guirao, L, Ritchie, H, Ortiz-Ospina, E and Roser, M, 'Life expectancy', 2023, ourworldindata.org/life-expectancy.

Introduction

Gallup, *State of the Global Workplace: 2024 Report*, 2024, gallup. com/workplace/349484/state-of-the-global-workplace.aspx.

Bailey, R, 'There are now 5 generations in the workforce – can they work together?', *Fast Company*, 7 February 2019, fastcompany. com/90302569/there-are-now-5-generations-in-the-workforce-can-they-work-together.

Chapter 1

Ducharme, J, 'The sunk cost fallacy is ruining your decisions. Here's how', *TIME*, 26 July 2018, time.com/5347133/ sunk-cost-fallacy-decisions/.

McDonald, J, 'Why Australians are working longer and retiring later', *Forbes Advisor*, 5 December 2023, forbes.com/advisor/au/ superannuation/australians-retiring-later-in-life/.

Orthia, L, Hosking, D and McCallum, J (2022), *'If people want to work they should be able to': Older Australians' Perspectives on Working After Retirement*, National Seniors Australia, 2022, nationalseniors.com.au/uploads/NSA-2022-Post-Retirement-Work-Report-Final.pdf.

Whiting, K, 'Want to live a long, healthy life? 6 secrets from Japan's oldest people', Health and Healthcare Systems, World Economic Forum, 29 September 2021, weforum.org/agenda/2021/09/japan-okinawa-secret-to-longevity-good-health/.

Mitsuhashi, Y, 'Ikigai: A Japanese concept to improve work and life', *BBC*, 8 August 2017, bbc.com/worklife/article/20170807-ikigai-a-japanese-concept-to-improve-work-and-life.

García, H and Miralles, F, *Ikigai: The Japanese secret to a long and happy life*, Random House UK, 2017.

Grant, A, 'Outsource inspiration' in Dutton, J and Spreitzer, G (eds), *How to Be a Positive Leader: Small actions, big impact*, Berrett-Koehler Publishers, 2014.

Harris, C, 'Building relationship currency in an isolated environment by Carla A. Harris', *LinkedIn Pulse*, 27 August 2020, linkedin.com/pulse/building-relationship-currency-isolated-environment-carla-harris/.

Chapter 2

Lencioni, PM, *The Ideal Team Player: How to recognize and cultivate the three essential virtues*, Jossey-Bass, 2016.

Seeber, C, 'Episode #18 – Let's Talk Performance with Emma Miller', *Eating Your Cake Too*, podcast, 2022.

Chapter 3

Goleman, D, 'The first component of emotional intelligence', in *Self-Awareness (HBR Emotional Intelligence Series)*, Harvard Business Review Press, 2018.

Di Battista, A, Grayling, S, Hasselaar, E, Leopold, T, Li, R, Rayner, M and Zahidi, S, *Future of Jobs Report 2023*, World Economic Forum, May 2023, weforum.org/docs/WEF_Future_of_Jobs_2023.pdf.

Eurich, T (2017), 'Increase your self-awareness with one simple fix', video, *TEDxMileHigh*, December 2017, youtube.com/watch?v=tGdsOXZpyWE.

Iscoe, K, 'Is being a high-achieving people-pleaser all bad? (nope, here's why)', *LinkedIn Pulse*, 22 February 2024, linkedin.com/pulse/being-high-achieving-people-pleaser-all-bad-nope-heres-iscoe-lkemc/.

Eurich, T, 'What self-awareness really is (and how to cultivate it)', in *Self-Awareness (HBR Emotional Intelligence Series)*, Harvard Business Review Press, 2018.

Hemingway, E, *The Sun Also Rises*, Scribner's, 1926.

Chand, SP, Kuckel, DP and Huecker, MR, *Cognitive Behavior Therapy*, StatPearls Publishing, 2022.

Dweck, C, *Mindset: Changing the way you think to fulfil your potential*, Little Brown, 2017.

Indeed Editorial Team, '84 types of values in the workplace (and how to choose), *Indeed*, updated 4 February 2023, indeed.com/career-advice/career-development/types-of-values.

Coelho, P, 'The fisherman and the businessman', Paulo Coelho: Stories and Reflections, 4 September 2015, paulocoelhoblog.com/2015/09/04/the-fisherman-and-the-businessman.

Chapter 4

Arruda, W, 'What Taylor Swift can teach you about your personal brand', *Forbes*, 5 February 2024, forbes.com/sites/williamarruda/2024/02/05/what-taylor-swift-can-teach-you-about-your-personal-brand/.

Clear, J, *Atomic Habits: An easy and proven way to build good habits and break bad ones*, Penguin Group, 2019.

Chapter 5

Ayto, J (ed), *From the Horse's Mouth: The Oxford Dictionary of English Idioms*, 3rd edn, Oxford University Press, 2010.

Harris, C, 'How to Find the Person Who Can Help You Get Ahead at Work', *TEDWomen 2018*, November 2018, ted.com/talks/carla_harris_how_to_find_the_person_who_can_help_you_get_ahead_at_work.

Maister, DH, Green, CH and Galford, RM, *The Trusted Advisor*, Touchstone, 2001.

Sinek, S, 'How great leaders inspire action' *TEDxPuget Sound*, September 2009, https://www.ted.com/talks/simon_sinek_how_great_leaders_inspire_action.

Chapter 6

Levitin, DJ, *The Organized Mind: Thinking straight in the age of information overload*, Dutton, 2014.

Hatton, SM, *Lead the Room: Communicate a message that counts in moments that matter*, Major Street Publishing, 2019.

Kilmann Diagnostics, 'Take the Thomas- Kilmann Conflict Mode Instrument (TKI)', accessed 19 June 2024, kilmanndiagnostics.com/overview-thomas-kilmann-conflict-mode-instrument-tki/.

Gallo, AE, 'The gift of conflict', TEDxBroadway, September 2019, ted.com/talks/amy_e_gallo_the_gift_of_conflict.

Earnshaw, E, *I Want This to Work: An inclusive guide to navigating the most difficult relationship issues we face in the modern age*, Sounds True, 2021.

Grayson Riegel, D, 'How to solicit negative feedback when your manager doesn't want to give it', *Harvard Business Review*, 5 March 2018, hbr.org/2018/03/how-to-solicit-negative-feedback-when-your-manager-doesnt-want-to-give-it.

Chapter 7

David, S, *Emotional Agility: Get unstuck, embrace change, and thrive in work and life*, Avery/Penguin Random House, 2016.

Taleb, NN, *Antifragile: Things that gain from disorder*, Random House, 2012.

The University of Queensland, 'How many career changes in a lifetime?', 19 June 2023, study.uq.edu.au/stories/how-many-career-changes-lifetime.

Broom, D (2023), 'Having many careers will be the norm, experts say', *Forum Institutional*, World Economic Forum, 2 May 2023, weforum.org/agenda/2023/05/workers-multiple-careers-jobs-skills/.

Dweck, C, *Mindset: Changing the way you think to fulfil your potential*, Little Brown, 2017.

In Time, motion picture, Niccol, A (dir.), 2011.

Bartlett, S, The Diary of a CEO: *The 33 laws of business and life*, Ebury Edge, 2023.

Hidden Figures, motion picture, Melfi, T (dir.), 2016.

Di Battista, A, Grayling, S, Hasselaar, E, Leopold, T, Li, R, Rayner, M and Zahidi, S, *Future of Jobs Report 2023*, World Economic Forum, May 2023, weforum.org/docs/WEF_Future_of_Jobs_2023.pdf.

Working with Claire

Working with Claire is not just about ticking boxes – it's about transforming your organisation from the inside out. Claire knows that her clients crave high-impact activities that ignite action at every level. Here's what happens when your organisation partners with Claire:

- **Enhanced talent retention.** Implement effective strategies to keep top talent engaged and committed reducing turnover rates and saving on recruitment costs.
- **Leadership development.** Equip your high-potential employees and leaders with the skills and knowledge necessary to inspire and manage a diverse, dynamic workforce – now and into the future.
- **Career advancement opportunities.** Invite more open dialogue and create clearer pathways for career progression, ensuring employees feel valued and motivated to grow within your organisation – and stay with it.
- **Increased reputational capital.** Enhance your organisation's reputation as a great place to work, attracting high-quality candidates and retaining a satisfied, engaged workforce through your ability to showcase the many ways you are investing in the growth of your people.

Through her workshops, programs and speaking opportunities, Claire's approach is practical and action-oriented, not just theoretical. She brings energy and an enthusiasm for ensuring organisations learn new insights and take action on them.

Get in touch with Claire via the following:

- claire@claireseeber.com.au
- www.linkedin.com/in/claireseeber
- www.instagram.com/eatingyourcaketoo
- www.facebook.com/eatingyourcaketoo

Be better with business books

————————————

MAJOR STREET

We hope you enjoy reading this book. We'd love you to post a review on social media or your favourite bookseller site. Please include the hashtag #majorstreetpublishing.

Major Street Publishing specialises in business, leadership, personal finance and motivational non-fiction books. If you'd like to receive regular updates about new Major Street books, email info@majorstreet.com.au and ask to be added to our mailing list.

Visit majorstreet.com.au to find out more about our books (print, audio and ebooks) and authors, read reviews and find links to our Your Next Read podcast.

We'd love you to follow us on social media.

in linkedin.com/company/major-street-publishing

f facebook.com/MajorStreetPublishing

○ instagram.com/majorstreetpublishing

✕ @MajorStreetPub